*FAVORITE NEW ORLEANS RECIPES*

# Favorite New Orleans Recipes

By

SUZANNE ORMOND
MARY E. IRVINE
DENYSE CANTIN

*Artwork by SUZANNE ORMOND*

PELICAN PUBLISHING COMPANY
GRETNA 1989

First printing, English edition, March 1979
First printing, French edition, March 1979
First printing, Spanish edition, March 1979
First printing, Trilingual edition, March 1979
Second printing, English edition, October 1979
Second printing, French edition, December 1980
Third printing, English edition, January 1981
Fourth printing, English edition, February 1983
Fifth printing, English edition, September 1984
Sixth printing, English edition, April 1986
Seventh printing, English edition, June 1987
Third printing, French edition, February 1989
Eighth printing, English edition, July 1989

Library of Congress Cataloging in Publication Data

Ormond, Suzanne.
    Favorite New Orleans recipes.

English, French, and Spanish.
    1. Cookery, American—Louisiana. 2. New Orleans—Social
life and customs. I. Irvine, Mary E., joint author. II. Cantin,
Denyse, joint author. III. Title.
TX 715.0735      641.5'9'76335      78-18841
ISBN: 0-88289-198-7

Manufactured in the United States of America

Published by Pelican Publishing Company, Inc.
1101 Monroe Street, Gretna, Louisiana 70053

# NUMBERED LIST OF RECIPES

**DRINKS**
1. Ramos Gin Fizz
2. Sazerac
3. Absinthe Frappé
4. Café Brûlot
5. Iced Coffee with Vanilla Ice Cream
6. Egg Nog
7. Café Au Lait

**APPETIZERS**
8. Oyster Cocktail
9. Shrimp Remoulade
10. Oysters Rockefeller
11. Oysters Louisiana
12. Oysters Bayou St. John
13. Oyster and Artichoke Ramekin
14. Molded Daube Glacé
15. Mock Hogshead Cheese

**SOUPS**
16. Oyster Stew
17. Oyster Soup
18. Turtle Soup
19. Shrimp Bisque
20. Crawfish Bisque
21. Seafood Gumbo
22. Gumbo Aux Herbes
23. Creole Oxtail Soup
24. Vegetable Soup
25. White Bean Soup
26. Peanut Butter Soup

## ENTRÉES, MEAT AND FOWL

27. Red Beans and Rice with Louisiana Smoked Sausage
28. Veal Shoulder Roast
29. Panéed Veal Cutlets
30. Grillades and Grits
31. Hot Daube and Spaghetti
32. Turkey with Oyster Stuffing
33. Creole Chicken Fricassée
34. Barbecued Wild Duck
35. Boned Ham with Dried Fruit Stuffing
36. Shrimp and Ham Jambalaya
37. Liver, Bacon, and Onions with Grits
38. Boiled Tongue with Caper Sauce

## ENTRÉES, FISH AND SHELLFISH

39. Redfish Courtbouillon
40. Poached Redfish
41. Cold Boiled Redfish with Mayonnaise Sauce
42. Redfish Pontchartrain
43. Fried Catfish
44. Trout Amandine
45. Broiled Stuffed Flounder
46. Crawfish Étouffée
47. Shrimp Creole
48. Barbecued Shrimp
49. Stuffed Shrimp
50. Shrimp Jambalaya
51. Oysters Brochette
52. Oyster Patties
53. Oyster Pie
54. Stuffed Crabs
55. Soft-Shell Crab Meuniere

## EGGS

56. Eggs Sudenmar
57. Eggs St. Denis
58. Eggs Sardou
59. Hard-Boiled Eggs with Cheese Sauce

## VEGETABLES

60. Dirty Rice
61. Brown Rice
62. Green Rice
63. Soufflées Potatoes
64. Candied Yams
65. Baked Bananas
66. Fried Ripe Plantains
67. Green Plantain Chips
68. Broiled Eggplant
69. Black-eyed Peas and Ham Hock
70. Stewed Okra, Corn, and Tomatoes
71. Mirlitons Stuffed with Ham and Shrimp
72. Cushaw
73. Skillet Cabbage
74. Boiled Beets and Greens
75. French Fried Broccoli
76. Stuffed Creole Tomatoes
77. Cheese Grits Casserole
78. Corn Pudding

## SALADS

79. Boiled Okra Salad
80. Mushroom Salad
81. Watercress Salad
82. String Bean Salad
83. Cucumber Salad (1)
84. Cucumber Salad (2)
85. Jerusalem Artichoke Salad

## DESSERTS

86. Bread Pudding
87. Rice Pudding
88. Cherries Jubilee
89. Bananas Foster
90. Banana Mousse
91. Ambrosia
92. Fresh Pineapple with Cream Cheese and Pecans

# ABBREVIATIONS

milliliter .......................... ml.
gram ................................ g.
kilogram .......................... kg.
centimeter ........................ cm.
millimeter ........................ mm.
ounce .............................. oz.
pound ............................. lb.
quart .............................. qt.
Centigrade ........................ C
Fahrenheit ........................ F

# PREFACE

Most New Orleanians, whether they are native born or transplanted, have a large collection of favorite recipes. With the publication of our book, *Louisiana's Art Nouveau: The Crafts of the Newcomb Style,* behind us, Mary E. Irvine and I turned our attention to the engrossing subject of New Orleans cooking.

Food is a favorite subject in New Orleans. People spend so much time debating the pros and cons of food that it seems a good part of one's waking time is consumed with the subject. Conversations center around whether this year's oysters are better than last, or whether the lack of or too much rain ruined the fig or tomato crop. But indeed, New Orleans has elevated the pleasures of cooking and consuming to highly skilled, sophisticated art forms. Now that transportation and refrigeration are available to everyone, our delicacies may be found in almost all market places, nationally and internationally. We can share our culinary heritage, now over two hundred and sixty years old.

Producing just another New Orleans cookbook seemed to us foolish, so we enlisted the aid of Denyse Cantin and set out to write a book in the three languages of the cultures Louisiana has experienced since 1718—French, Spanish, and English. These three cultures have tempered our cuisine, each adding its flavor to the native foods, until today the refinement is perfect.

Having made this decision, we looked through our files and notes for the best of the recipes. Many were only handwritten notes, some dating back to the middle of the nineteenth century; others were hastily jotted ingredients. In our own kitchens we cook by rote, never measuring, weighing, or timing. Therefore, we had to recreate from memory to produce proper quantities and yield, and we added the metric system.

We have carefully chosen recipes which may be done anywhere, adding some new favorites, and have written directions to make each recipe easy to follow. We have balanced the categories to make the book simple but complete, so that all, from gourmet chef to neophyte cook, may prepare and enjoy the food we consider the best in the world.

SUZANNE ORMOND

# FAVORITE NEW ORLEANS RECIPES

# Drinks

## • 1 •

### *RAMOS GIN FIZZ*

1½ oz. (45 ml.) dry gin
2 egg whites
2½ teaspoons (12.5 ml.) very fine
  or powdered sugar
2 oz. (60 ml.) light cream
3 drops Orange Blossom water

Juice of ½ lemon, strained
Juice of ½ lime, strained
Vanilla to taste
Crushed ice
10-oz. (300-ml.) tumbler

Mix all ingredients in blender, and mix at highest speed for a few seconds. Mixture must be thick but fluffy (airy). If too thin, blend more. The drink can also be mixed with rotary beater, being sure to blend it well. Sparkling water can also be added. Serves 1.

## SAZERAC

1 to 2 oz. (30 to 60 ml.) Bourbon
or Rye whiskey
2 teaspoons (10 ml.) fine sugar
or 2 sugar cubes
½ teaspoon (2.5 ml.) Peychaud
bitters or Tabasco

Few drops Angostura bitters
1 teaspoon (5 ml.) Herbsaint or
Pernod
1 lemon zest
Ice cubes
Old-fashioned glass

Mix all ingredients except Herbsaint or Pernod and lemon zest in shaker. Cool glass with ice cubes. Pour Herbsaint or Pernod, turn glass in all directions to coat it with liqueur. Empty glass. With spoon, gently mix ingredients in shaker. Do not stir. Strain into glass and add lemon zest. Serves 1.

## ABSINTHE FRAPPÉ

1½ oz. (45 ml.) Pernod or
Herbsaint
½ teaspoon (2.5 ml.) fine sugar

Crushed ice
Champagne glass

Cool cocktail shaker and champagne glass with crushed ice. In the shaker mix other ingredients to dissolve sugar, and pour into cooled champagne glass. Water or sparkling water may be added to taste. Serves 1.

# CAFÉ BRÛLOT

Peel of 1 orange in one continuous strip
Peel of 1 lemon, thinly sliced
6 whole cloves
3 large sugar cubes
1 cinnamon stick, 2 inches (5 cm.) long
½ cup (125 ml.) Cognac
¼ cup (60 ml.) Curacao or other orange liqueur
1 chafing dish or Café Brûlot bowl
2 cups (500 ml. or ½ liter) very strong black coffee

Heat the chafing dish over low heat. Rub orange peel with sugar cubes before slicing to absorb the zest. Put in chafing dish with the next 4 ingredients. Slightly mash with back of spoon. Add Cognac and Curacao and mix well. When mixture is hot, ignite and flambé a few seconds, stirring constantly. Slowly add coffee until flame dies. Serve immediately. Serves 6.

# ICED COFFEE WITH VANILLA ICE CREAM

32 oz. or 1 qt. (1 liter) dark roast coffee with chicory
1 qt. (1 liter) vanilla ice cream
2 oz. (60 ml.) Cognac or Brandy
10-oz. (300-ml.) tumblers
Brew coffee and allow it to get lukewarm at room temperature.

In a punch bowl, pour coffee, half of ice cream, and 2 oz. (60 ml.) brandy or cognac. With a rotary beater, beat until mixture gets bubbly. Add remaining ice cream so that it floats in center. Serve in punch cups or double old-fashioned glasses. Serves 6.

## EGG NOG

1 qt. (1 liter) whole milk
4 large eggs, separated
½ cup (125 ml.) sugar

1 qt. (1 liter) vanilla ice cream
4 oz. (125 ml.) Bourbon whiskey
Freshly ground nutmeg

Scald milk. Beat egg yolks and sugar together until creamy and light in color. Pour a small amount of scalded milk into egg mixture, stir well, and reverse procedure. Cook over very low heat until well blended. Remove and cool. Beat egg whites until very stiff.

Into a punch bowl, pour milk and egg mixture. Gently fold in whiskey and egg whites. Float ice cream in center. Garnish top with freshly ground nutmeg. Serves 6.

## CAFÉ AU LAIT

3 cups (750 ml.) very strong
  coffee
3 cups (750 ml.) hot milk

or
2½ cups (625 ml.) hot milk and ½
  cup (125 ml.) light cream

Heat milk (or milk and cream) to just below boiling point and beat with rotary beater until foamy. Fill bowl or large cup with milk and coffee, pouring at same time and with equal quantity. Sugar to taste. Serves 6.

# Appetizers

• 8 •

## OYSTER COCKTAIL

Oysters can be served on a bed of shredded lettuce in individual bowls with a remoulade sauce or the following:

| | |
|---|---|
| 3 doz. oysters | ¼ cup (60 ml.) chili sauce |
| 2 tablespoons (30 ml.) mayonnaise | ¼ cup (60 ml.) ketchup |
| | Celery salt |
| 2 tablespoons (30 ml.) fresh lemon juice | Tabasco to taste |

Mix mayonnaise with lemon juice until well blended. Add other ingredients and chill.

NOTE: See Shrimp Remoulade (# 9) for sauce recipe. Serves 6.

# SHRIMP REMOULADE

3 doz. boiled, peeled, deveined, and chilled shrimp

1 head iceberg lettuce, shredded

**SAUCE**

¼ cup (60 ml.) Creole or Horseradish mustard
1 tablespoon (15 ml.) paprika
½ teaspoon (2.5 ml.) Cayenne red pepper
1 tablespoon (15 ml.) salt
3 tablespoons (45 ml.) tomato ketchup
6 tablespoons (90 ml.) Tarragon vinegar

4 tablespoons (60 ml.) fresh lemon juice, strained
1½ cups (375 ml.) olive oil
½ cup (125 ml.) green onions, chopped
½ cup (125 ml.) celery, chopped
2 sprigs fresh parsley, chopped
6 slices of lemon

Mix dry ingredients in bowl. Add mustard, ketchup, and blend. Beat in vinegar. Then slowly add oil in a thin stream, whisking constantly. Add finely chopped vegetables and lemon juice. Arrange shrimp on lettuce. Spoon sauce over. Garnish with lemon slices.

NOTE: This sauce can be made in a blender. Mix all ingredients except shrimp, and blend until well mixed.

NOTE: This sauce can be used over oysters.

Serves 6.

## OYSTERS ROCKEFELLER

3 doz. freshly shucked oysters
  on half shell
1 bunch spinach
1 bunch green onions
1 bunch parsley
1 small head lettuce
Green leaves of 1 head of celery

1 pound (450 g.) butter
1 tablespoon (15 ml.) Lea and
  Perrin Worcestershire sauce
1 tablespoon (15 ml.) absinthe
Salt and pepper to taste
Bread crumbs
Parmesan cheese

In a food processor, grind leaves together and mix well with butter. Add Worcestershire sauce, absinthe, salt, and pepper. Refrigerate paste to harden. When ready to serve, drain oysters and place in half shells, put a teaspoon of paste on each oyster, sprinkle with bread crumbs and Parmesan cheese. Set oysters on bed of rock salt and broil in metal pie pan for 8 minutes, 3 inches (8 cm.) from heat. Serves 6.

## OYSTERS LOUISIANA

3 doz. freshly shucked oysters
  on half shell
½ pound (225 g.) medium-sized
  fresh mushrooms, quartered
8 tablespoons (4 oz./113 g.) butter
4 tablespoons (60 ml.) flour
2 to 3 garlic pods, chopped fine
1 large bunch green onions,
  chopped fine

¼ cup (60 ml.) celery, chopped
  fine
¼ cup (60 ml.) fresh parsley,
  chopped fine
⅓ cup (80 ml.) dry sherry
Garlic salt
Fine bread crumbs

Drain oysters and reserve liquor. In skillet, sauté mushrooms in 2 tablespoons (28 g.) butter. Set aside. In another skillet, melt 5 tablespoons (70 g.) butter, add flour; mix well, stirring constantly over low heat. Cook slowly until golden color. Add green onions, celery, parsley, garlic, and cook a few minutes until vegetables are tender. Add garlic salt, sherry, and mix well. Add oysters, mushrooms, and some of oyster liquor. Simmer over low heat a few minutes, until oysters begin to curl. Divide mixture into 6 individual buttered baking dishes or shells. Sprinkle with bread crumbs. Dot with butter and bake 15 minutes in 350°F (175°C) oven (or 4-5 on the thermostat). Serves 6.

## OYSTERS BAYOU ST. JOHN

36 medium raw oysters
6 tablespoons (90 ml.) foie gras

Breadcrumbs
6 scallop shells

Drain oysters, reserve liquor, and pat dry. It is important that this be done at first to have oysters very dry when ready to use.

SAUCE

6 tablespoons (3 oz./88 g.) butter
6 tablespoons (90 ml.) flour
2 beef bouillon cubes
¾ cup (175 ml.) heavy whipping
  cream
¾ cup (175 ml.) chicken bouillon

¼ to ½ cup (60 ml. to 120 ml.)
  oyster liquor
Salt and pepper
Few drops of lemon juice
Few drops of Tabasco
1 teaspoon (5 ml.) dry parsley

In a heavy skillet melt butter and blend in flour. Cook a few minutes over low heat, stirring. Add beef cubes. Stir until dissolved. Remove from heat, slowly add the liquid ingredients and the seasonings. Stir well to blend, making sure that the sauce is smooth. Return to heat, continue to stir until mixture becomes very thick. Remove from heat.

Divide oysters equally in buttered shells. Dot with ½ teaspoon (2.5 ml.) of foie gras per oyster. Pour sauce over to cover all the oysters. Sprinkle generously with bread crumbs. Broil in oven about 8 inches (20 cm.) from heat for about 4 minutes.

NOTE: This is a new recipe prepared especially for this book. The name comes from the famous bayou in New Orleans. The dish was made for the first time in the kitchen of Denyse Cantin, about fifty feet (15 meters) from the bayou. Because of its great new flavor we named it for Bayou St. John and hope that history will treat us with the same kindness. Happy eating! Serves 6.

## OYSTER AND ARTICHOKE RAMEKIN

3 large artichokes
1 teaspoon (5 ml.) salt
18 large raw oysters with liquor
6 large fresh mushrooms, sliced
2 tablespoons (30 ml.) minced
  onion

1 tablespoon (15 ml.) minced
  parsley
½ stick (2 oz./56 g.) butter
2 tablespoons (30 ml.) flour
Salt and pepper to taste

Place artichokes in large saucepan with 2 inches (5 cm.) water and 1 teaspoon (5 ml.) salt. Bring to rapid boil and lower heat to simmer. Cover pot and cook for about 45 minutes or until bottoms are tender but firm. Drain and allow to cool. Remove bottoms and cut into 1-inch (2.5-cm.) cubes. Scrape leaves. Set aside.

In heavy cold skillet, lightly brown flour and set aside. In another heavy skillet, sauté onion and mushrooms in butter until lightly browned, about 5 minutes. Remove from heat. Add browned flour and parsley. Mix well. Slowly pour in oyster liquor and simmer 10 minutes. Season to taste. Drop oysters into hot mixture and allow edges to curl. Remove from heat. Keep warm. In 6 ramekins, divide artichokes and scrapings equally. Pour oyster and mushroom mixture over and bake in 350°F (175°C) oven (4-5 on the thermostat) for 10 to 15 minutes. Serves 6.

## MOLDED DAUBE GLACÉ

5 cups (1.25 liters) beef
  consommé
1 pound (450 g.) roast beef or
  boiled beef
1 cup (250 ml.) water
6 tablespoons (90 ml.)
  unflavored gelatin
4 ribs celery, chopped
1 carrot, chopped
2 onions, chopped

1 green pepper, chopped
2 tablespoons (30 ml.) cider
  vinegar
Juice of 1 lemon
4 teaspoons (20 ml.) salt
½ teaspoon (2.5 ml.) Cayenne
  pepper
¼ teaspoon (1.25 ml.) Tabasco
1½ teaspoons (7.5 ml.)
  Worcestershire sauce

To the consommé, add all ingredients except gelatin and meat. Bring to a boil; simmer uncovered about 10 minutes. Strain in colander. Reserve consommé. Dissolve gelatin in 1 cup (250 ml.) cold water; add to consommé and heat to dissolve. Shred meat and mix with consommé. Mold in loaf pan. Refrigerate for 4 hours or until gelatin is set. Serves 12.

# MOCK HOGSHEAD CHEESE

1 beef or pork tongue
3 pounds (1.5 kg.) fresh pork
  shoulder
2 fresh pork feet
1 teaspoon (5 ml.) salt
½ teaspoon (2.5 ml.) pepper
3 cloves garlic
1 cup (250 ml.) onions, chopped
3 sprigs parsley

1 cup (250 ml.) chopped celery
½ chopped bell pepper
1 tablespoon (15 ml.) unflavored
  gelatin
2 cups (500 ml.) cider vinegar
1 bunch green onions, chopped

Clean tongue under cold water. Cut pork into small chunks. Put
tongue into large pot with parsley, celery, onions, seasonings, and
cover with water. Cook 1 hour. Add cubed pork and pork feet.
Cook 2 hours more until meat falls apart; drain and reserve stock.
Let meat cool. Peel tongue; pull meat apart and discard bones.
Shread meat; add vinegar, green pepper, and green onions; and
mix well. Put into 3 loaf pans, filling to a depth of 1½ inches (3
cm.). Dissolve gelatin in some meat broth and add to enough stock
to cover meat in each loaf pan. Refrigerate overnight. Cut into
square or slices. Serve cold. Serves 12.

# Soups

## *OYSTER STEW*

2 doz. whole oysters
1 doz. cut-up oysters
2 tablespoons (1oz./28 g.) butter
4 green onions or 1 onion, chopped
1 tablespoon (15 ml.) flour
2 ribs celery with leaves, chopped
2 tablespoons (30 ml.) green pepper, chopped

1 cup (250 ml.) oyster liquor or tap water
Dash of thyme, marjoram, and paprika
1 teaspoon (5 ml.) salt
¼ teaspoon (1.25 ml.) pepper
1 bay leaf (remove before serving)
2 tablespoons (30 ml.) parsley
2 cups (500 ml.) hot milk

In heavy skillet, sauté onion, celery, and green pepper in butter until lightly brown. Sprinkle flour and blend well. Slowly blend in oyster liquor. Stir until well blended. Add seasoning and one dozen oysters cut up, and simmer uncovered over low heat for half an hour. When ready to serve, add the two dozen whole oysters. Cook until edges curl. Add hot milk. Serve at once.

NOTE: With oyster crackers and a salad, this can be served as a main course. Serves 6.

## OYSTER SOUP

3 doz. oysters freshly opened,
and oyster liquor
3 cups (750 ml.) milk
¾ cup (175 ml.) cream

¼ cup (2 oz./56 g.) butter
1 teaspoon (5 ml.) salt
Dash of pepper

Mix milk and cream, and heat to scalding. Set aside. In a separate pot, melt butter, add oyster liquor, and heat. Add oysters. Cook gently until oyster edges curl. Add to scalded milk and cream. Season with salt and pepper. Heat without boiling. Serve immediately with oyster crackers. Serves 6.

## TURTLE SOUP

1 pound (450 g.) fresh turtle
meat
8 cups (2 liters) water
1 teaspoon (5 ml.) salt
6 peppercorns
2 green onions, chopped
1 rib celery, chopped
1 large onion, finely chopped
1 clove garlic, minced
1 tablespoon (15 ml.) parsley,
minced

½ stick (2 oz./56 g.) butter
2 tablespoons (30 ml.) flour
½ cup (125 ml.) strained
tomatoes
Salt and pepper to taste
2 hard-boiled eggs
1 lemon, cut into 6 slices
Dry sherry

In a 12-cup (3-liter) saucepan, put turtle meat, water, salt, peppercorns, green onions, and celery. Boil for 45 minutes, covered. Skim often to keep clear. Remove meat, drain broth, and set aside.

In a heavy cast-iron covered saucepan (12-cup/3-liter size), make brown roux with flour and butter. Add onion, parsley, garlic, and tomatoes. Over low heat, simmer about 10 minutes. Add turtle meat and broth, and continue to simmer covered for about 1½ hours, or until turtle meat is tender. Add salt and pepper. Chop hard-boiled eggs and set aside.

Place hot turtle soup in a soup tureen and garnish with egg and lemon slices. Ladle soup out into bowls and add about an ounce (35 ml.) of sherry to each serving. Serves 6.

# SHRIMP BISQUE

2 pounds (1 kg.) shrimp, fresh or frozen, shelled and deveined
½ pound (8 oz./250 g.) butter, melted
½ teaspoon (2.5 ml.) ground red pepper
½ teaspoon (2.5 ml.) salt
1 teaspoon (5 ml.) garlic salt
1 teaspoon (5 ml.) barbecue spice

1 teaspoon (5 ml.) paprika
1½ teaspoons (7.5 ml.) Worcestershire sauce
Lemon slices
1 large Spanish onion, chopped
1 tablespoon (15 ml.) cornstarch
½ cup (125 ml.) whipping cream

Rinse shrimp well and pat dry. Put in a baking dish with first 8 ingredients. Mix well. Cook in 300°F (150°C) oven (2 on thermostat), basting occasionally for 30-40 minutes. Cool and refrigerate until butter comes to the surface and hardens. In a skillet, melt the shrimp butter and add the chopped onion. Cover and simmer until very tender. With a slotted spoon, remove a few shrimp and set aside to garnish. When the onion is tender, puree in a blender along with the sauce and rest of shrimp. Pour in the top of a double boiler. Add cornstarch diluted with cold water. Cook until thick. Add whipping cream. Heat and serve. Garnish with shrimp.

NOTE: This is the same recipe as Barbecued Shrimp (# 48), and it can be made in the same manner with the leftovers. Serves 6.

# CRAWFISH BISQUE

10 pounds (4.5 kg.) live crawfish
2 large onions, quartered
Parsley sprigs
Lemon slices
Salt
Boiling water to cover

In container of cold water with 1 cup (250 ml.) salt, soak crawfish for a few minutes to purge. Rinse well until water is clear. Drop live crawfish into boiling water, with onions, parsley, lemon slices, and 2 tablespoons (30 ml.) salt. Cook 10 minutes and drain on absorbent paper. Reduce boiling water to 2 quarts (2 liters). Strain and reserve. Separate heads from tails. Peel tails and put aside. Clean about 40 to 50 heads for stuffing, reserving fat in separate container. Divide fat and tails equally for bisque and stuffing.

**BISQUE**
½ cup (125 ml.) cooking oil
1 stick (4 oz./113 g.) butter
1 cup (250 ml.) flour
2 cloves garlic, chopped fine
1 large onion, chopped fine
1 bell pepper, chopped fine
3 to 4 celery ribs and leaves,
   chopped fine

½ cup (125 ml.) tomato paste
Reserved crawfish water or
   plain water, about 2 quarts (2
   liters)
4 chopped green onion tops
Dry parsley to garnish
Salt and Cayenne pepper

Make brown roux with butter, oil, flour. Add next 5 ingredients. Cook, stirring frequently, until vegetables are soft. Add half of crawfish tails and half of fat. Cook very slowly about 20 minutes. Gradually add reserved liquid and seasoning. Simmer until consistency of thick soup, about 20 to 30 minutes. Just before serving add green onion tops, parsley, and baked stuffed crawfish heads. Serve over rice.

**HEADS**
Reserved half crawfish tails
Reserved crawfish fat
40 to 50 cleaned crawfish heads
4 oz. (113 g.) butter
½ cup (125 ml.) oil
2 large onions, chopped fine
1 bell pepper, chopped fine

¾ cup (175 ml.) water
1½ cups (375 ml.) fresh bread
   crumbs
Parsley
Green onion tops
2 garlic cloves, chopped
Salt and red pepper to taste
Flour

Grind crawfish tails; heat oil and butter. Add onions and bell pepper. Cook until soft. Add tails and fat. Simmer another 15 minutes. Add bread crumbs, seasoning, green onion tops, parsley, garlic, and water. Mix well. Stuff heads. Roll in flour and bake in 350°F (175°C) oven (4-5 on the thermostat) about 10 minutes. Serves 6 to 8.

NOTE: (Crawfish tails, butter, and cleaned heads can be bought in fish market or groceries. This reduces work and preparation time.)

• 21 •

## SEAFOOD GUMBO

2 pounds (1 kg.) fresh shrimp, peeled and deveined
6 small whole fresh or frozen crabs, outside shell removed
1 pound (450 g.) claw crabmeat
4 pounds (2 kg.) okra
6 tablespoons (90 ml.) cooking oil
3 large red onions, chopped
5 ribs celery, chopped
1 green pepper, chopped
8 cups (2 liters) water
2 teaspoons (10 ml.) thyme, ground
2 whole bay leaves (remove before serving)
2 teaspoons (10 ml.) salt
1 teaspoon (5 ml.) Cayenne pepper
1 teaspoon (5 ml.) black pepper
6 cups (1.5 liters) hot boiled rice

Wipe okra with dry cloth to remove fuzz. Cut and discard stem ends, and slice ¼ inch (6.35 mm.) thick. On very slow heat, in 2 heavy skillets with 2 tablespoons (30 ml.) oil in each pan, fry okra until dry, stirring frequently. In a third skillet, in 1 tablespoon (15 ml.) oil, sauté onion, celery, and green pepper until limp. Add to okra. Transfer mixture into soup pot, add water and seasonings, and simmer partly covered, stirring occasionally for 3 to 4 hours. Add hot water if necessary.

In heavy skillet in 1 tablespoon (15 ml.) oil, slightly sauté shrimp until pink. Clean crabs and split in two. Add shrimp, crabs, and crabmeat to boiling soup; stir, and continue cooking 15 to 20 minutes longer.

Serve with a mound of hot rice and half a crab in each serving. Offer French bread and butter and a combination salad for a total meal. Serves 12.

## GUMBO AUX HERBES

1 small white cabbage, shredded
1 bunch of each of the following: beet leaves, turnip leaves, mustard leaves, spinach, watercress, and parsley
5 large green onions, chopped
1 large white onion, chopped

¼ pound (113 g.) veal brisket, cubed
One ½-inch (12.7-mm.) slice cooked ham, cubed
1 teaspoon (5 ml.) baking soda
1 tablespoon (15 ml.) cooking oil
Salt and pepper
3 cups (750 ml.) hot boiled rice

Thoroughly wash all greens, including green onions, in salted water, removing sand and grit. In large soup kettle with one inch (2.5 cm.) of water and baking soda, bring water to boil and lower heat. Place greens a few at a time, letting them cook down slowly. Greens will make their own liquid. Continue process until all greens are in pot. Simmer uncovered 1 hour. Cool and chop. In large skillet, sauté veal, ham, and white onion in cooking oil until brown. Add salt and pepper. Replace chopped greens in kettle, add meat mixture, and mix well. Add enough boiling water to cover slightly. Let gumbo come to a boil and cook until liquid is reduced to half. Check seasoning and serve over hot boiled rice. Serves 6.

## CREOLE OXTAIL SOUP

2 tablespoons (30 ml.) cooking oil
2 oxtails, cut into pieces
3 carrots in chunks
1 large onion
4 celery ribs with leaves, in chunks
2 leeks in chunks
1 turnip in chunks
4 tomatoes, peeled and chopped, or 1 16-oz. (450-g.) can tomatoes

1 bay leaf (remove before serving)
2 sprigs parsley
3 cloves, stuck in onion
1 teaspoon (5 ml.) salt
½ teaspoon (2.5 ml.) Cayenne pepper
1 teaspoon (5 ml.) black pepper
Water
Dry sherry (optional)

Put oil in soup kettle over medium heat. When warm, add vegetables and oxtail pieces; cover and brown slowly about 20 minutes, stirring occasionally to prevent burning. Add all other ingredients except sherry. Cover and simmer 3 to 4 hours until meat is tender and easily pulled away from bones. Serve a piece of oxtail in each plate, with some sherry to taste. Serves 6.

## VEGETABLE SOUP

5 pounds (2.5 kg.) beef chuck
2 large beef soup bones
6 large carrots, sliced thin
2 large white onions, coarsely
  chopped
2 large turnips, coarsely
  chopped
4 ribs celery, coarsely chopped
One 2-pound (1-kg.) head
  cabbage, shredded
2 large tomatoes, peeled,
  chopped and seeded
2 large white potatoes, cut in
  cubes

2 tablespoons (30 ml.) salt
12 peppercorns
½ teaspoon (2.5 ml.) crushed red
  pepper
1 bay leaf (remove before
  serving)
2 teaspoons (10 ml.) thyme
  leaves
6 large whole white potatoes,
  peeled
Water

In a large soup kettle, place all ingredients, except whole potatoes, with enough water to cover generously. Let liquid boil rapidly, then lower heat to simmer. Skim when necessary. Continue to cook until meat is very tender, about 2 hours.

Place whole potatoes in soup broth and boil for 15 minutes. Remove meat and potatoes. Keep warm. Serve soup broth and vegetables in bowls as first course. Slice meat and serve with potatoes as an entrée with horseradish sauce.

### HORSERADISH SAUCE

8 oz. (250 ml.) sour cream
3 tablespoons (45 ml.)
  horseradish

2 teaspoons (10 ml.)
  Worcestershire sauce

Blend well. Serves 6 to 8.

## WHITE BEAN SOUP

1 pound (450 g.) dry Navy beans,
soaked at least 6 hours
½ pound (225 g.) dry salt pork or
1 large ham bone with meat
10 cups (2.5 liters) water
1 large onion, cut in half
2 carrots, in large chunks
1 potato, cut in half
2 celery ribs with leaves, in
chunks

1 bay leaf (remove before
serving)
Minced parsley
¼ teaspoon (1.25 ml.) savory
Pinch of ground thyme
Pepper
1 smoked sausage (optional)

Drain beans. In large pot or kettle, put all ingredients except smoked sausage. Cover and simmer 3 to 4 hours. Beans must be very tender and soup thick. If sausage is added, slice and fry slowly to render fat. Add to soup 1 hour before end of cooking time. Add seasoning, if necessary; sprinkle with parsley. Serves 6.

## PEANUT BUTTER SOUP

4 tablespoons (2 oz./56 g.) butter
3 ribs celery, chopped fine
1 large onion, chopped fine
2 tablespoons (30 ml.) flour
5 cups (1.25 liters) chicken stock
1½ cup (375 ml.) smooth peanut
butter, room temperature
½ cup (125 ml.) whipping cream

¼ teaspoon (1.25 ml.) celery salt
1 teaspoon (5 ml.) salt
¼ teaspoon (1.25 ml.) white
pepper
Few drops lemon juice
Chopped peanuts or crumbled
bacon (optional)

In a heavy pot, melt butter over moderate heat. Add celery, onion, and simmer covered about 20 minutes or until vegetables are limp, stirring occasionally. Add flour, mix well, blend in chicken stock. Stirring constantly, bring to a boil over medium heat until thick and smooth. Reduce heat and simmer uncovered another 20 minutes. Purée in blender. In large bowl, put peanut butter and gradually whisk in stock; mix well until smooth, and return to pot. Add cream, seasonings, and heat thoroughly. (Do not boil.) Sprinkle with chopped peanuts or crumbled bacon. Serves 6.

# Entrees, meat and fowl

## RED BEANS AND RICE
## WITH LOUISIANA SMOKED SAUSAGE

1 pound (450 g.) dried red
  kidney beans
1 ham bone or ham hock
1 large onion, chopped fine
½ cup (125 ml.) celery with tops,
  chopped fine
1 large clove garlic, minced
2 tablespoons (30 ml.) parsley,
  minced

1 large bay leaf (remove before
  serving)
6 drops Tabasco
Salt to taste
8 to 10 cups (2 to 2.5 liters) water
1 pound (450 g.) smoked
  sausage cut in 2-inch (5 cm.)
  pieces
3 cups (750 ml.) hot boiled rice

Soak beans 6 hours in enough water to cover. Drain and discard water. In 12-cup (3-liter) covered saucepan, place all ingredients except sausage and rice, and cook over medium heat about 20 minutes or until a brisk boil occurs. Lower heat to simmer. Cover and cook about 1½ hours or until beans are soft. Remove about 15 beans and mash; return them to pot and allow to cook another 15 minutes, uncovered. Add smoked sausage and cook until done, about 10 minutes. Serve over hot boiled rice. Serves 6 to 8.

## VEAL SHOULDER ROAST

5-pound (2.25-kg.) veal shoulder roast, boned
2 large loaves white bread
3 tablespoons (1½ oz./42 g.) butter
2 medium onions, chopped
4 tablespoons (60 ml.) parsley, chopped fine
1 cup (250 ml.) celery, chopped fine
1 cup (250 ml.) milk
3 eggs, beaten
1 pound (450 g.) pork sausage meat
½ pound (225 g.) fresh mushrooms, chopped
Salt and pepper to taste
¼ teaspoon (1.25 ml.) thyme leaves

Make pocket in veal for stuffing. Remove and discard crust from bread. Soak bread in milk. In 2 tablespoons (28 g.) butter, sauté onions, parsley, and celery until limp and golden. Drain bread and add to mixture. In another skillet, in remaining butter, sauté pork sausage meat and mushrooms until brown, and drain. Mix with bread mixture. Add eggs and seasonings; cook slightly. Fill veal pocket with stuffing and sew with large needle and cotton thread. Roast in 325°F (165°C) oven (3 on the thermostat) for 3½ hours. Serves 10.

## PANÉED VEAL CUTLETS

6 veal cutlets, ¼ inch (5 mm.) thick
1 cup (250 ml.) toasted bread crumbs
1 egg, beaten with 1 tablespoon (15 ml.) water
Salt and pepper
Cooking oil and butter
Lemon wedges

Pound veal with mallet until thin and tender. Salt and pepper meat. Dip meat in egg mixture and dredge in crumbs. Dip meat a second time and dredge. In heavy skillet, heat ½ inch (1.5 cm.) oil and butter to very hot. Lower heat and sauté meat until brown on both sides. Drain on absorbent paper. Serve with lemon wedges. Serves 6.

## GRILLADES AND GRITS

2 pounds (1 kg.) beef or calf round, about ½ inch (1.5 cm.) thick
3 tablespoons (45 ml.) cooking oil
Salt, pepper, and flour
1 large onion, thinly sliced
2 cloves garlic, minced
1 small green pepper, chopped fine
1 cup (250 ml.) tomatoes, chopped

1 tablespoon (15 ml.) parsley
⅛ teaspoon (0.5 ml.) thyme leaves
2 tablespoons (30 ml.) flour
1½ cups (375 ml.) water
Salt and pepper
1 drop Tabasco
3 cups (750 ml.) hot, cooked, buttered grits

Cut meat into 2-inch (5-cm.) squares and season with salt and pepper. Dredge with flour. In large heavy skillet, heat 2 tablespoons (30 ml.) cooking oil. When oil is hot, brown meat lightly. Remove and drain on absorbent paper. Set aside.

In heavy skillet, make roux with 2 tablespoons (30 ml.) flour and 1 tablespoon (15 ml.) cooking oil. Brown roux until a rich dark color. Add all other ingredients except grits and simmer about 15 minutes, stirring until mixture thickens. Boil briskly. Lower heat to simmer and add meat. Cover skillet and allow to cook about 1 hour or until gravy is thick and meat is tender, stirring often. Serve over hot buttered grits. Serves 6.

## HOT DAUBE AND SPAGHETTI

3- to 4-pound (1.5 kg. to 2 kg.)
beef round roast
Cooking oil, salt, pepper, and
flour
4 medium onions, thinly sliced
1 small green pepper, thinly
sliced
4 small fresh tomatoes, peeled
and thinly sliced
1 large bay leaf (remove before
serving)

½ teaspoon (2.5 ml.) rosemary
leaves
1 clove garlic, minced
2 tablespoons (30 ml.) parsley,
minced
Salt and pepper to taste
4 drops Tabasco
Water
½ lb. (225 g.) boiled, buttered,
thin spaghetti

Dredge meat in salt, pepper, and flour. Place small amount of oil in heavy cast-iron pot, deep enough to cover size of roast with ample room. Heat oil until hot, and brown roast until a thick crust appears. Remove roast and drain on absorbent paper. Pour off oil, leaving about one tablespoon (15 ml.). Lightly sauté onions, tomatoes, and green peppers. Return roast to pot with enough water to barely cover. Place all other ingredients except spaghetti in pot and let come to full boil. Lower heat, cover, and simmer about 2 hours or until roast is done but stays firm. Add seasoning if desired. Add to gravy a mixture of 1 tablespoon (15 ml.) flour and 1 tablespoon (15 ml.) melted butter to thicken. Continue to cook for 20 minutes longer. Remove meat and slice. Serve over hot buttered spaghetti. Serves 6 to 8.

# TURKEY WITH OYSTER STUFFING

One 10-pound (5-kg.) turkey
½ Spanish onion, chopped fine
2 bell peppers, chopped fine
1 large bunch green onions,
chopped fine
3 to 4 celery hearts, chopped
fine
1 clove garlic, chopped fine
Crumbs of 18 slices fresh white
bread
Liver, gizzard, and heart of
turkey, chopped fine
3 doz. small oysters, drained,
reserving liquor

½ pound (225 g.) fresh
mushrooms, quartered
½ stick (4 oz./113 g.) butter
2 eggs, slightly beaten
Extra gizzards, livers, necks (¼
pound/113 g. of each) for
gravy
3 cups (750 ml.) chicken
bouillon
2 tablespoons (30 ml.) sugar
4 tablespoons (60 ml.) water
Salt, pepper, chopped parsley,
poultry seasoning

**STUFFING**

Melt butter and gently sauté onions, bell peppers, celery, green onion, and garlic, about 3 minutes. Add mushrooms. Cook a few minutes longer. Add liver, gizzards, and oysters and cook a few minutes. Remove from heat; add half the bread crumbs and about 2 tablespoons (30 ml.) oyster liquor. Mix well but carefully. Cook 3 minutes longer. Remove from heat. Add rest of bread crumbs, beaten eggs, seasoning, and more oyster liquor until desired consistency. Mix well. Stuff turkey.

Heat oven to 400°F (205°C) (5-6 on the thermostat). Place additional gizzards, livers, necks in bottom of roasting pan and roast for about 1 to 1½ hours. Remove excess fat, grease. Brush turkey with softened butter; sprinkle salt, pepper, and paprika. Place on rack on top of roasted giblets. Set oven to 450°F (235°C) (6-7 on the thermostat) for the first half hour. Reduce to 325°F (165°C) (3 on the thermostat). Cover and roast for 3 hours. Remove cover and continue to roast for last half hour.

**GRAVY**

In small skillet, put 2 tablespoons (30 ml.) sugar with 4 tablespoons (60 ml.) water and cook on high heat until it caramelizes. Remove from heat; add chicken bouillon mixture. Stir until caramel dissolves. Keep warm. When cooked, place turkey on warm platter. Remove rack and pour off excess grease. On medium heat, add chicken bouillon mixture. Simmer slowly. Thicken with arrowroot, if desired. Serves 6 to 8.

# CREOLE CHICKEN FRICASSÉE

One 2- to 3-pound (1- to 1.5-kg.)
fryer chicken, cut in 6 pieces
Cooking oil, salt, pepper, and
flour
1 large onion, chopped fine
1 clove garlic, minced
2 tablespoons (30 ml.) parsley,
minced
½ cup (125 ml.) celery, finely
chopped
1 large bay leaf (remove before
serving)

1 cup (250 ml.) tomatoes,
chopped
2 cups (500 ml.) water
1 tablespoon (15 ml.) cooking oil
1 tablespoon (15 ml.) flour
Salt and pepper to taste
2 drops Tabasco
3 cups (750 ml.) hot boiled rice

Salt, pepper, and flour chicken pieces. In heavy cast-iron skillet, place enough cooking oil to cover bottom, about ½ inch (1.5 cm.). When oil is hot, add chicken pieces and brown to dark golden color. Remove from skillet and drain on absorbent paper. In a 12-cup (3-liter) saucepan, make a roux with 1 tablespoon (15 ml.) flour and 1 tablespoon (15 ml.) oil. Stir roux until dark brown in color, keeping heat low so that burning does not occur. Add onion, parsley, celery, garlic, tomatoes, bay leaf, and water. Stir until mixture thickens and comes to a brisk boil, about 20 minutes. Season to taste, and add Tabasco. Add browned chicken parts and cover. Lower heat until slow simmer occurs. Cook about 1 hour or until chicken is tender. Serve over hot boiled rice. Serves 6.

# BARBECUED WILD DUCK

3 wild ducks
3 small onions, cut in half
3 celery ribs, in big chunks
20-oz. (580-g.) can of cubed
   pineapple, drained, juice
   reserved
3 small garlic pods

Slices of fresh pork or bacon
Salt and pepper
Worcestershire sauce
Giblets from ducks
½ pound (225 g.) chicken livers,
   gizzards, and necks

Wash and dry ducks. Sprinkle inside with salt, pepper, few drops Worcestershire sauce. Inside cavity, place onion, celery, garlic, and pineapple. Wrap pork or bacon around duck. Tie with string and put on spit of barbecue. Prepare hot fire with charcoal on each side of brazier. In center, put a container of double foil with ½ cup (125 ml.) water, and giblets from ducks and chickens. Cook 1 to 1½ hours depending on size, basting regularly with the following sauce.

## SAUCE

¼ cup (60 ml.) honey
Reserved pineapple juice

2 tablespoons (30 ml.) Soy sauce
½ cup (125 ml.) crab apple jelly

Mix well, heat, and simmer a few minutes. When ducks are ready, place on warm platter and keep in oven. Take foil container off brazier, add water, and stir, scraping all clinging pieces. Empty in saucepan; remove gizzards, necks, and hearts. With fork or blender purée liver; add to sauce. Heat. Serve on ducks. Serves 6.

## BONED HAM WITH DRIED FRUIT STUFFING

One 8- to 12-pound (4- to 6-kg.)
ham, cooked, boned
1 pound (450 g.) mixed dried
fruit
3 cups (750 ml.) water
1 cup (250 ml.) sugar

1 tablespoon (15 ml.) lemon
juice
1 tablespoon (15 ml.) cornstarch
1 cup (250 ml.) fresh bread
crumbs
¼ cup (60 ml.) rum

Make pocket in ham for stuffing. Soak fruit in a bowl with water
for 2 to 3 hours. Drain and reserve water. In a saucepan, place
reserved water with sugar and cook for 5 minutes to dissolve. Add
lemon juice and cornstarch, cooking and stirring until mixture
thickens. Remove from heat and cool. Add rum, fruit, and bread
crumbs. Mix well and stuff ham. Bake ham in 325°F (165°C) oven
(3 on the thermostat) for 3 hours. Serves about 20.

## SHRIMP AND HAM JAMBALAYA

2 pounds (1 kg.) shrimp, peeled
and deveined
1 cup (250 ml.) ham, coarsely
chopped
1 green bell pepper, finely
chopped
½ cup (125 ml.) celery, finely
chopped
2 cups (500 ml.) fresh or canned
tomatoes, chopped

1 large onion, finely chopped
1 clove garlic, minced
2 tablespoons (30 ml.) parsley,
minced
6 teaspoons (1 oz./28 g.) butter
1 bay leaf (remove before
serving)
3 cups (750 ml.) hot boiled rice
1 teaspoon (5 ml.) salt
6 drops Tabasco

In heavy skillet, melt 4 teaspoons (20 g.) butter over low heat and
sauté green pepper, celery, onion, and parsley until limp and golden brown. Add tomatoes, garlic, and bay leaf. Stir constantly.
Add salt and Tabasco; cook until mixture begins to boil. Lower
heat and simmer for 20 minutes, stirring until mixture thickens.

In another skillet, with 2 teaspoons (10 g.) butter, lightly sauté
shrimp and ham. When shrimp are firm and light pink, transfer
to tomato sauce. Allow to cook about 5 minutes.

Add rice; stir to blend until rice is well coated and has absorbed
tomato sauce. Serve at once. Serves 6.

## *LIVER, BACON, AND ONIONS WITH GRITS*

12 slices bacon
6 large slices calves' liver, ¼ inch (0.5 cm.) thick

3 large onions, sliced thin
2 cups (500 ml.) hot cooked grits
1 stick (4 oz./113 g.) butter

In a skillet fry bacon until crisp. Remove and drain on absorbent paper. Keep warm. Sauté onion in bacon fat until golden. Remove from fat and keep warm. Fry liver on both sides. Pour a bit of hot water in pan, lower heat, and simmer for 3 minutes. Add onion and cook one minute longer. Transfer to platter, placing bacon slices on top. Serve with grits and butter. Serves 6.

## *BOILED TONGUE WITH CAPER SAUCE*

3 small calves' tongues
3 carrots, in large chunks
1 small rutabaga, in chunks
1 large onion, cut in 4 pieces
4 celery ribs with leaves, broken in pieces

1 bay leaf (remove before serving)
2 whole cloves
1 large garlic pod
Salt, pepper, celery salt, M.S.G.

Place all ingredients in large pot. Cover with cold water with 1 inch (2.5 cm.) over. Cover and simmer 3 to 3½ hours, depending on size of tongues. Peel. Slice and keep warm. Drain and reserve stock.

### CAPER SAUCE

6 tablespoons (3 oz./84 g.) butter
6 tablespoons (90 ml.) flour

2 cups (500 ml.) bouillon from tongues
4 tablespoons (60 ml.) capers

In heavy skillet, melt butter, add flour and cook, stirring, until a golden brown roux appears. Cool a few minutes, stirring, and add stock. Stir until blended. Cook on moderate heat, stirring until thickened. Add capers. Season to taste. Serve over sliced tongue. Serves 6.

NOTE: This stock makes a wonderful soup.

NOTE: Vegetables used for seasoning stock may be discarded; replace with fresh vegetables of your choice and serve with meat.

# Entrees, fish and shellfish

## *REDFISH COURTBOUILLON*

6 slices redfish, ½ inch (1.5 cm.) thick, cleaned and scaled
¾ cup (175 ml.) flour
½ cup (125 ml.) oil
1 medium onion, chopped fine
1 bell pepper, chopped fine
3 celery ribs and leaves, chopped fine
1 clove garlic, minced
1 bunch green onions, chopped fine
16-oz. (450-g.) can peeled tomatoes, chopped
1 cup (250 ml.) tomato paste

Fresh minced parsley
½ teaspoon (2.5 ml.) thyme
¼ teaspoon (1.25 ml.) marjoram
¼ teaspoon (1.25 ml.) allspice
½ teaspoon (2.5 ml.) Cayenne pepper
2 tablespoons (30 ml.) lemon juice
½ cup (125 ml.) dry red wine
1 bay leaf (remove before serving)
Salt and pepper
3 cups (750 ml.) water
Lemon slices

• ENTREES, FISH AND SHELLFISH •

Make dark brown roux with flour and oil. (Takes about 20 minutes of slow cooking, stirring constantly.) Add next five ingredients and cook 5 to 10 minutes until vegetables are soft. Add tomatoes and tomato paste. Mix well. Add all other ingredients except fish. Bring to boil, stirring constantly. Lower heat and cook slowly, uncovered, until very thick (about 25 to 30 minutes). Put fish in the sauce, turning to coat well. Add lemon slices. Cover. Reduce heat to lowest setting, letting sauce just barely simmer for 10 to 15 minutes, or until fish flakes easily. Serve redfish with sauce spooned over. Serves 6.

· 40 ·

## POACHED REDFISH

2 whole redfish, medium sized (5 pounds/2.5 kg.), scaled, heads removed
5 celery tops, with leaves cut into chunks
2 medium onions, quartered
1 carrot, sliced fine
4 sprigs parsley
8 cups (2 liters) milk
4 cups (1 liter) water
7 slices lemon
Salt, pepper, celery salt

Wash and dry fish. In cavity, place half a small onion, celery leaves, parsley and 1 lemon slice. Wrap in cheesecloth and tie. Make courtbouillon with all ingredients except fish. Simmer, covered, 20 minutes or until vegetables are cooked. Remove with slotted spoon. Put fish on rack in courtbouillon and cover. Bring to a boil, lower heat, and poach 20 to 25 minutes, or until fish flakes easily. If courtbouillon does not cover fish, turn once while poaching. Remove to heated platter. Keep warm. Drain and reserve liquid.

### SAUCE

1½ sticks (6 oz./168 g.) butter
12 tablespoons (180 ml.) flour
6 hard-boiled eggs, coarsely chopped
Lemon juice

Melt butter. Add flour. Mix well. Cook a few minutes. Remove from heat, stir in 6 cups (1.5 liters) reserved liquid. Mix well. Cook until thick, adding more liquid if too thick. Stir in eggs and a few drops lemon juice into sauce. Season to taste. Serve over fish. Garnish with other lemon slices. Serves 6.

# COLD BOILED REDFISH WITH MAYONNAISE SAUCE

6-pound (3.5-kg.) whole redfish,
scaled, with head and tail on
1 large onion, cut in half
3 ribs celery
1 large carrot, cut in half
5 sprigs parsley

¼ teaspoon (1.25 ml.) each:
rosemary, crushed red
pepper, thyme leaves
1 teaspoon (5 ml.) black pepper
1 tablespoon (15 ml.) salt

Place fish in pan large enough to hold it. Put all ingredients into pan, with just enough water to cover. Poach fish until meat flakes away from center bone, about 15 minutes. Cool. Drain water from fish and reserve. Discard all seasonings. Place cool fish on platter, removing skin and bone, but replacing meat, head and tail to resemble whole fish. Reduce reserved liquid to half, and pour small amount over fish to form gelatin. Refrigerate for 24 hours.

## MAYONNAISE SAUCE

2 cups (500 ml.) fresh
mayonnaise
6 oz. (180 ml.) chow chow
6 hard-boiled eggs, chopped
coarsely
2 tablespoons (30 ml.) drained
capers

1 teaspoon (5 ml.) salt
¼ teaspoon (1.25 ml.) white
pepper
3 drops Tabasco

In bowl, combine all ingredients well, but do not beat. Pour mayonnaise over cold fish. Serves 6 to 8.

## REDFISH PONTCHARTRAIN

6 redfish steaks, 1 inch (2.5 cm.) thick, deboned
1 cup (250 ml.) fresh crabmeat
6 large fresh mushrooms, sliced
2 green onions, minced
2 tablespoons (30 ml.) melted butter

2 tablespoons (30 ml.) lemon juice
4 tablespoons (2 oz./56 g.) butter
Salt and pepper
6 lemon wedges

Salt and pepper fish on both sides and place in shallow baking dish. Brush top with melted butter and lemon juice. Place under broiler about 3 inches (8 cm.) from heat. Broil 10 minutes. In skillet, put 4 tablespoons (56 g.) butter; sauté mushrooms, onions, and crabmeat for 5 minutes. Set aside. When fish is broiled on one side, turn and brush with more lemon juice and butter. Replace and broil for 5 minutes. Spoon crabmeat mixture over redfish. Continue to broil for 5 minutes. Serve with lemon wedges. Serves 6.

## FRIED CATFISH

2 pounds (1 kg.) catfish, sliced thin
2 eggs, separated
2 tablespoons (30 ml.) water
1 cup (250 ml.) cracker crumbs

Salt
Pepper
6 tablespoons (90 ml.) cooking oil or peanut oil

Salt and pepper fish. Beat egg whites stiff and fold in beaten egg yolks and water. Spread cracker crumbs on two plates and season with salt and pepper. Coat catfish slices in seasoned bread crumbs, dip in egg mixture, and again in cracker crumbs. In heavy skillet, fry in hot oil 2 minutes; turn and fry one minute. Remove from frying pan and drain on absorbent paper. Serve with the following sauce.

### SAUCE FOR CATFISH

2 tablespoons (30 ml.) mayonnaise
1 tablespoon (15 ml) fresh lemon juice

½ cup (125 ml.) ketchup
¼ cup (60 ml.) whipping cream
Celery Salt

Mix mayonnaise with lemon juice until well blended. Add all other ingredients and mix well. Serves 6.

# TROUT AMANDINE

6 medium speckled trout filets, or 6 small trout with heads and tails
Cold milk for soaking
Seasoned flour (salt and pepper)

1 stick (4 oz./113 g.) butter or ½ stick (2 oz./56 g.) butter and 2 oz. (60 ml.) cooking oil

Soak fish in cold milk for about 10 minutes. Drain; roll in seasoned flour. Shake off excess. Melt butter in heavy frying pan and fry fish a few at a time, depending on size, 5 minutes each side, until cooked golden and crisp. Place on warm platter. Keep warm.

## SAUCE

¾ stick (3 oz./84 g.) butter
1½ cups (375 ml.) flaked blanched almonds

¼ cup (60 ml.) fresh lemon juice
Parsley
Salt and pepper

In same skillet, melt butter and lightly brown almonds. Add lemon juice, parsley, and seasonings. Simmer gently to reduce. Pour sauce over fish. Serves 6.

# BROILED STUFFED FLOUNDER

6 medium-sized fresh flounder
3 tablespoons (45 ml.) melted
butter

3 tablespoons (45 ml.) lemon
juice

Wash and dry fish; split them from thick side length-wise to form pocket for stuffing. Put three cross-wise slashes into skin on top side of fish.

## STUFFING

1 cup (250 ml.) coarse fresh
bread crumbs
½ cup (125 ml.) celery, finely
chopped
½ cup (125 ml.) green onion with
tops, finely chopped
½ cup (125 ml.) cooked shrimp,
coarsely chopped

½ cup (125 ml.) cooked lump
crabmeat
1 tablespoon (15 ml.) parsley,
minced
½ stick (2 oz./56 g.) butter
1 egg, beaten with 1 teaspoon (5
ml.) milk
Salt and pepper

In large, heavy skillet, place butter. When melted and bubbly, sauté onions, celery, and parsley until light golden and limp. Add shrimp, crabmeat, and bread crumbs. Mix well. Pour egg and milk mixture over ingredients and blend well, keeping heat low. Salt and pepper to taste. Remove from heat, and cool enough to manipulate. Divide mixture into 6 parts. Stuff each fish. Place fish in shallow baking dish and brush with melted butter and lemon juice. Broil 3 inches (8 cm.) from heat until skin of fish is brown and flakes easily. Serves 6.

## CRAWFISH ÉTOUFFÉE

1½ sticks (6 oz./168 g.) butter
½ cup (125 ml.) crawfish fat, if available
¼ cup (60 ml.) flour
2 large onions, chopped
1 large bell pepper, chopped fine
2 ribs celery and leaves, chopped fine
2 garlic cloves, minced
White pepper and salt

¼ teaspoon (1.25 ml.) Cayenne pepper
1 to 2 cups (250 to 500 ml.) water
2 pounds (1 kg.) shelled crawfish tails, fresh or frozen
1 tablespoon (15 ml.) lemon juice
Minced green onions and parsley
3 cups (750 ml.) hot boiled rice

Make medium brown roux with butter and flour. Add onion, bell pepper, celery, garlic, and crawfish fat if used. Cook, stirring frequently, until vegetables are tender and light brown (about 30 minutes). Add crawfish tails, seasoning, lemon juice. Mix well. Gradually add water, according to desired thickness. Bring to boil, lower heat. Simmer covered until tails are tender. Add green onions and parsley and serve over rice. Serves 6.

## SHRIMP CREOLE

2 pounds (1 kg.) shrimp, peeled and deveined
1 large green pepper, chopped fine
1 medium onion, chopped fine
2 ribs celery, chopped fine
2 tablespoons (30 ml.) parsley, minced
1 large bay leaf (remove before serving)
2 cups (500 ml.) tomatoes, chopped

1 teaspoon (5 ml.) Worcestershire sauce
½ teaspoon (2.5 ml.) thyme leaves
½ teaspoon (2.5 ml.) sugar
3 tablespoons (1½ oz./43 g.) butter
2 tablespoons (30 ml.) flour
1 teaspoon (5 ml.) salt
6 drops Tabasco

In large, heavy skillet, melt 2 tablespoons (28 g.) butter over low heat. Sauté onion until limp but not brown. Push onion to one side and add flour, stirring until brown. Add all other ingredients except shrimp. Stir constantly until mixture thickens and comes to slow boil. Lower heat until mixture simmers, cover, and continue to cook for about 35 minutes. In another skillet, in 1 tablespoon (14 g.) butter, lightly sauté shrimp until they are firm and light pink. Add to gravy and continue to simmer for 10 minutes. Serve over hot boiled rice. Serves 6.

• 48 •

## BARBECUED SHRIMP

4 pounds (2 kg.) fresh or frozen large shrimp with tails, heads, and shells (20 to 25 in one pound/0.5 kg.)
4 sticks (1 pound/450 g.)butter
¾ teaspoon (3.75 ml.) ground red pepper
¾ teaspoon (3.75 ml.) salt

2 teaspoons (10 ml.) garlic salt
2 teaspoons (10 ml.) barbecue spice
2 teaspoons (10 ml.) paprika
3 teaspoons (15 ml.) Worcestershire sauce
Lemon slices

Rinse shrimp well, cover with cold water with 2 teaspoons (10 ml.) salt and 1 lemon, sliced. Refrigerate 1 hour. Drain and pat dry; put in shallow baking dish.

### SAUCE
In saucepan, melt butter on low heat. Add all other ingredients. Mix well. Do not boil.

Pour over shrimp. Add lemon slices. Cook in 300°F (148°C) oven (2 on the thermostat), basting occasionally, for 30 to 40 minutes, until shell pulls away from meat. Serve with orzo or rice and French bread. Serve shrimp in large soup bowls with sauce ladled over for dunking. Serves 6.

## *STUFFED SHRIMP*

3 dozen jumbo raw shrimp
4 tablespoons (60 ml.) chopped
  bell pepper
3 ribs celery, chopped
1 large onion, chopped
1 small clove garlic, pressed
1 stick (4 oz./113 g.) butter
6 slices white bread, soaked in
  ¼ cup (60 ml.) milk
2 eggs, beaten
½ pound (225 g.) crabmeat
¾ cup (175 ml.) raw shrimp,
  chopped

2 teaspoons (10 ml.) salt
1 teaspoon (5 ml.) black pepper
¼ cup (60 ml.) fresh parsley,
  chopped
3 to 4 drops Tabasco
Pinch of celery salt and garlic
  salt
Flour
2 eggs, beaten with ½ cup (125
  ml.) milk
Cooking oil
Bread crumbs

Peel large shrimp, keeping tails. Butterfly by splitting down back, almost but not all the way through. Devein. Sauté onions, celery, bell pepper, and garlic in butter until vegetables are limp and tender. Squeeze bread dry, and add with beaten eggs. Cook a few minutes, stirring constantly, until mixture thickens. Add chopped shrimp and cook until tender but firm. Add crabmeat and seasoning. Heat gently, stirring constantly. Stuff slit shrimp with mixture and refrigerate at least 12 hours, or freeze until hard. Dip shrimp in flour, then in egg and milk mixture and in bread crumbs. Fry in deep hot fat 360°F (182°C) until golden brown, 4 or 5 minutes.

NOTE: Oysters can be used instead of chopped shrimp. Serves 6.

## SHRIMP JAMBALAYA

4 large onions, chopped
3 cloves garlic, chopped fine
2 pounds (1 kg.) large fresh
   shrimp, peeled and deveined
2 cups (500 ml.) raw
   long-grained rice

3 cups (750 ml.) water
½ cup (125 ml.) chopped green
   onion tops
Cooking oil
Salt
Red and black pepper to taste

In large heavy skillet, put enough oil to cover bottom. Sauté onions and garlic until limp and golden. Add shrimp and water. Heat to simmer and cook for 10 minutes. Wash rice, and add to shrimp mixture with green onions, salt, and pepper. Toss lightly, and cook rapidly until most water is gone and rice begins to puff. Lower heat, cover, and cook approximately 20 minutes or until rice is cooked and shrimp are tender but firm. Serves 6.

## OYSTERS BROCHETTE

36 medium-sized oysters,
   freshly shucked
10 slices thick bacon, cut in
   1½-inch (4 cm.) squares
1 stick (4 oz./113 g.) butter
⅓ cup (80 ml.) olive oil

Fresh parsley, minced
1 teaspoon (5 ml.) lemon juice
Flour
Pinch of black pepper
12 toasted bread triangles

In deep skillet, sauté bacon squares until partially cooked; drain on absorbent paper. Dry oysters. On skewers, alternate bacon and oysters, allowing 6 per person. Roll in flour seasoned with pepper. In heavy skillet, melt butter and oil, fry brochettes, turning them until lightly browned. Serve on toasted bread triangles with parsley and lemon juice or with the following.

### SAUCE

1 stick (4 oz./113 g.) butter
2 tablespoons (30 ml.) lemon
   juice

1 tablespoon (15 ml.)
   Worcestershire sauce
Paprika

Combine all ingredients and heat. Serves 6.

## OYSTER PATTIES

6 large patty shells, baked, with top circle removed and hollowed out; reserve tops
36 medium fresh shucked oysters with liquor
1 large onion, chopped fine
2 tablespoons (30 ml.) cooking oil
2 tablespoons (30 ml.) flour
1 teaspoon (5 ml.) garlic juice

2 tablespoons (30 ml.) parsley, minced
1 teaspoon (5 ml.) Worcestershire sauce
½ teaspoon (2.5 ml.) salt
¼ teaspoon (1.25 ml.) black pepper
⅛ teaspoon (0.5 ml.) thyme leaves
Water

In a heavy cast-iron skillet over low heat, combine oil and flour and stir until blended and light brown color appears. Add onions and continue to cook, stirring constantly until dark rich brown color appears. Remove from heat. Drain oysters in colander and reserve liquor. Return skillet to very low heat, and pour in oyster liquor. Add garlic, parsley, thyme, Worcestershire sauce, salt, and pepper. Cook slowly, adding just enough water to keep roux pasty looking. Stir constantly. Add oysters and cook gently until they begin to puff and edges start to curl. Remove from heat. Divide oyster mixture equally into 6 shells. Replace tops. Place in shallow baking dish and bake in 350°F (175°C) oven (4-5 on the thermostat) for 15 to 20 minutes or until patty shells are hot and crisp. Serves 6.

# OYSTER PIE

36 medium oysters with liquor
2 tablespoons (30 ml.) flour
2 tablespoons (30 ml.) cooking
  oil
1 medium onion, chopped fine
3 ribs celery, chopped fine
3 tablespoons (45 ml.) parsley
½ cup (125 ml.) bell pepper,
  chopped fine

2 cloves garlic, chopped fine
1 teaspoon (5 ml.) salt
¼ teaspoon (1.25 ml.) fresh
  ground black pepper
4 drops Tabasco
½ pound (225 g.) fresh pork
  sausage meat
Flour

Make small balls of pork sausage. Roll in flour. In heavy skillet, brown sausage and drain on absorbent paper. Set aside. In another skillet, make roux with cooking oil and flour to light brown. Add onions, celery, green pepper, and parsley. Lower heat. Continue to cook, stirring, until vegetables are limp. Add salt, pepper, and Tabasco. Stir. Add oysters and liquor and cooked pork sausage balls. Blend well. Remove from heat.

## PIE CRUST

2 cups (500 ml.) flour
1 teaspoon (5 ml.) salt
2/3 cup (160 ml.) shortening or
  lard

5 to 6 tablespoons (75 to 90 ml.)
  ice water

In mixing bowl, sift flour and salt. Cut in shortening with pastry blender. Sprinkle with water. Mix well. Divide pastry ⅔ and ⅓. Roll out on floured board.

Line 8-cup (2-liter) casserole or soufflé dish with ⅔ pastry dough. Pour in oyster mixture. Cover with ⅓ pastry dough. Seal edges. Cut steam vent in top. Bake in 450°F (235°C) oven (6-7 on the thermostat) 15 minutes; lower heat to 350°F (175°C) (4-5 on the thermostat); cook 30 minutes longer, or until crust is brown. Serves 6.

## STUFFED CRABS

6 fresh live hard-shelled crabs
1 large onion, chopped fine
4 green onions, chopped fine
1 stick (4 oz./113 g.) butter
2 cups (500 ml.) coarse fresh
  bread crumbs
¼ cup (60 ml.) milk
2 tablespoons (30 ml.) parsley,
  minced

½ teaspoon (2.5 ml.) salt
½ teaspoon (2.5 ml.) black
  pepper
½ cup (125 ml.) fine toasted
  bread crumbs
Butter

Place live crabs in large pot of boiling water, adding 1 tablespoon (15 ml.) of salt to 4 quarts (4 liters) water. Boil crabs for 20 minutes or until bright red. Remove from water and cool. When cool enough to handle, remove big top shell carefully. Clean thoroughly and set aside. Remove meat by picking from all parts of crab, making sure no shell fragments remain in meat. In heavy skillet, melt butter over medium heat and sauté onion and green onions until limp and golden. Add bread crumbs and milk and stir. Lower heat and cook about 3 minutes or until milk is well blended into mixture. Add parsley, crabmeat, salt, and pepper; blend and cook for 2 minutes. Remove from heat and allow to cool slightly. Divide stuffing equally between the 6 shells by stuffing mixture tightly and mounding over top. Sprinkle with toasted bread crumbs and dot with butter. Place stuffed crab shells in shallow pan and bake in 350°F (175°C) oven (4-5 on the thermostat) for 15 minutes. Serves 6.

## SOFT-SHELL CRAB MEUNIERE

6 large soft-shell crabs  
½ stick (2 oz./56 g.) butter  
Milk for soaking

Salt and pepper  
Flour

Wash crabs and remove deadmen from gill area. In shallow dish, place crabs; cover with fresh whole milk. Allow to soak for 30 minutes. Drain but do not dry. Salt and pepper and dredge in flour until well coated.

In heavy skillet, melt butter over low heat. When butter begins to bubble, add crabs and sauté gently on top shell side until golden brown, about 7 to 10 minutes. Turn crabs and repeat sauté process until golden brown and firm. Remove and add enough water to make thick gravy. Pour over crabs. Serves 6.

## *EGGS SUDENMAR*

6 bread casings

2 dozen medium shrimp, fresh or frozen, shelled, deveined, cut in two

2 dozen whole small oysters, drained

6 eggs

6 tablespoons (90 ml.) caviar

**BREAD CASINGS**

6 slices French bread, 1 inch (2.5 cm.) thick, 4 to 6 inches (10 to 15 cm.) in diameter

3 tablespoons (45 ml.) melted butter

Carefully remove the crust from bread. Form a hole halfway through in the center. Coat well, all sides, with melted butter using a pastry brush. Set aside.

## SAUCE

1 tablespoon (14 g.) butter
2 tablespoons (30 ml.) carrots,
  chopped fine
2 tablespoons (30 ml.) green
  onions, chopped fine
2 tablespoons (30 ml.) celery,
  chopped fine
2 tablespoons (30 ml.) white
  onions, chopped fine

1 tablespoon (15 ml.) flour
½ cup (125 ml.) white wine
2 tablespoons (30 ml.) tomato
  paste
1 cup (250 ml.) hot milk
Salt and pepper
1 cup (250 ml.) whipping cream
Few drops Tabasco

In a heavy saucepan, melt butter, add all vegetables, and cook slowly for 3 minutes. Remove from heat and mix in flour and tomato paste. Add wine, milk, and blend into mixture with a wire whisk. Add salt and pepper. Return to medium heat and cook about 10 minutes. Add cream, Tabasco, and cook on high heat stirring occasionally for 20 minutes. Keep warm.

In a heavy skillet melt 1 tablespoon (14 g.) butter, and lightly sauté shrimp until pink. Add oysters and continue to cook until edges start to curl. Add to sauce. Heat oven 350°F (175°C) (4-5 on the thermostat). Place bread casings on a cookie sheet on center shelf and cook 10 minutes.

TO ASSEMBLE: Poach eggs in normal way. Place bread casings on a large platter or individual plates. Place the poached eggs in center hole; pour seafood sauce over and top with one tablespoon (15 ml.) caviar.

NOTE: This is a new recipe. We have chosen to call it in our honor: Suzanne (SU), Denyse (DEN), and Mary (MAR). We hope you like it as well as we do. We had such fun making this new dish and happily share it with you. Good eating! Serves 6.

## EGGS ST. DENIS

½ cup (125 ml.) ham, chopped
fine
1 cup (250 ml.) raw chicken
livers, chopped fine
½ cup (125 ml.) fresh
mushrooms, chopped
coarsely

½ teaspoon (2.5 ml.) olive oil
2 tablespoons (1 oz./28 g.) butter
2 cups (500 ml.) brown sauce
6 slices toast, edges trimmed
6 large eggs

In large skillet, sauté ham, chicken livers, and mushrooms in butter and olive oil until brown. Remove and drain on absorbent paper.

### BROWN SAUCE

1 onion, minced
2 tablespoons (1 oz./28 g.) butter
2 tablespoons (30 ml.) flour
3 cups (750 ml.) beef stock

½ cup (125 ml.) tomato purée
3 oz. (90 ml.) sherry
½ teaspoon (2.5 ml.) salt
4 drops Tabasco

In large, heavy skillet, melt butter and lightly sauté onions until. limp and golden. Add flour and make dark brown roux. Stir constantly. Slowly add stock, and purée until all is blended. Lower heat and cook for about 20 minutes, stirring constantly, until mixture thickens and reduces by about half. Add sherry, salt, and Tabasco. Add chicken liver and ham mixture and continue to cook about 5 minutes. Arrange toast in bottom of shallow baking dish. In large skillet, break eggs one at a time and fry in small amount of butter on both sides. Transfer eggs when cooked to toast in pan. Pour hot sauce over and place in 350°F (175°C) oven (4-5 on the thermostat) for about 10 minutes. Serves 6.

# EGGS SARDOU

6 poached eggs
6 artichoke bottoms, heated in
  butter
6 toasted muffin rounds
1 box frozen chopped spinach

1 cup (250 ml.) thick bechamel
  sauce
1 cup (250 ml.) hollandaise
  sauce

Cook spinach in salted water. Drain, pressing with spoon to dry completely.

**BECHAMEL SAUCE**

3 tablespoons (43 g.) butter
3 tablespoons (45 ml.) flour
6 oz. (175 ml.) evaporated milk

¾ cup (175 ml.) whole milk
Pepper

In saucepan, melt butter and add flour. Mix well. Cook a few minutes stirring without browning. Remove from heat. Add evaporated milk and whole milk. Cook over moderate heat until very thick. Add spinach, pepper. Mix well. Keep warm.

**HOLLANDAISE SAUCE**

½ cup (4 oz./113 g.) butter
½ cup (125 ml.) whipping cream
2 egg yolks, beaten until thick
  and pale color

1 tablespoon (15 ml.) lemon
  juice
Salt and pepper

Heat butter and cream in top of double boiler about one hour. When ready to serve, beat egg yolks again with lemon juice, salt, and pepper. Add to butter and cream mixture. Stir 2 or 3 minutes until thick. Keep warm. (Caution: Water must be kept below boiling point.)

TO ASSEMBLE: Place muffin in plate; cover with creamed spinach. Put artichoke bottom on top, and cover with poached egg. Spoon hollandaise sauce over. Serves 6.

# HARD-BOILED EGGS WITH CHEESE SAUCE

6 eggs
½ cup (125 ml.) milk
½ cup (125 ml.) cream

1 tablespoon (15 ml.) flour
¼ pound (4 oz./113 g.) sharp
Cheddar cheese, grated

Hard cook eggs in the following manner: place unshelled eggs in glass or enamel saucepan; cover with cold water. Put over medium heat and bring water to boiling point. Reduce heat and simmer for 15 minutes. Plunge eggs in cold water. Shell and cut in half lengthwise. Set aside. In saucepan, beat flour, milk, and cream with wire whisk. Heat gently, stirring frequently. Add cheese a little at a time, stirring constantly until melted and mixture has thickened. Place layer of eggs, cut side up, in serving dish; salt lightly. Pour half cheese mixture over eggs. Repeat procedure until all is used. Keep warm. Serves 6.

# Vegetables

## DIRTY RICE

½ to 1 stick (2 to 4 oz./56 to 113 g.) butter
1 large onion, chopped fine
2 large garlic cloves, chopped fine
Bunch of green onions, chopped fine (6 or 7)
½ lb. (225 g.) each chicken gizzards and livers, minced
1 cup (250 ml.) raw long-grained rice
2 cups (500 ml.) water or chicken stock
Salt, pepper, garlic salt, parsley

In heavy skillet, melt butter. Gently sauté onion, garlic, and green onions until soft but not brown (about 3 to 4 minutes). Add minced gizzards and livers and cook until firm. Put mixture in saucepan. Add rice. Mix well. Add water or chicken stock and simmer about 20 minutes. Season to taste. Serves 6.

## BROWN RICE

1½ cups (375 ml.) raw
  long-grained rice
3 cups (750 ml.) beef or chicken
  consommé
8 tablespoons (4 oz./113 g.)
  butter

1 large onion, sliced
¼ teaspoon (1.25 ml.) thyme
  leaves
¼ teaspoon (1.25 ml.) marjoram
¼ teaspoon (1.25 ml.) rosemary

In skillet, brown rice in butter. Put in baking dish with other ingredients. In 350°F (175°C) oven (4-5 on the thermostat), bake rice, covered, for ½ hour. Uncover, stir, and bake ½ hour or until all liquid is absorbed.

NOTE: Do not use instant or any rapid cooking rice. Serves 6.

## GREEN RICE

1½ cups (375 ml.) raw white rice,
  washed twice
3 tablespoons (45 ml.) cooking
  oil
1 cup (250 ml.) celery, minced
¼ cup (60 ml.) parsley, minced

¼ cup (60 ml.) green onions,
  minced
½ teaspoon (2.5 ml.) salt
⅛ teaspoon (0.5 ml.) thyme
  leaves
3 cups (750 ml.) chicken stock

In heavy skillet, heat oil and add rice. Fry rice until light in weight and golden. Add all other ingredients except stock and gently sauté. Add stock and lower heat. Stir thoroughly. Cover tightly. Cook for 20 minutes. Uncover and steam until all liquid is absorbed. Serves 6.

## SOUFFLÉES POTATOES

12 medium-sized potatoes
Oil for deep frying

2 skillets for deep frying, with
wire basket

Peel potatoes. Cut lengthwise into slices ⅛ inch (3.17 mm.) thick. Wash and dry on cloth. A few at a time, plunge into deep hot—but not too hot—fat (365°F/180°C), gradually heating fat, and cook until potatoes begin to rise to surface, about 7 minutes. Drain in basket. Plunge again in the other pan of oil, heated at 375°F (188°C). Potatoes should be puffed immediately. Drain on absorbent paper. At that stage, potatoes can wait indefinitely. At time of serving, reheat potatoes in hot oil, drain on absorbent paper, and add salt. Serves 6.

## CANDIED YAMS

6 large Louisiana yams, peeled
  and sliced into rounds
6 tablespoons (3 oz./84 g.) butter
1 cup (250 ml.) sugar

2 lemons, sliced thin
2 tablespoons (30 ml.) lemon
  juice

In skillet, let butter come to bubble, and sauté yams until golden brown. As each slice browns, remove it to casserole dish, alternating with lemon slices. Continue until all yams are browned. Add sugar and lemon juice to skillet, scraping all clinging bits. Simmer, stirring, until syrup forms. If too thick, add small amount of water to thin. Pour sugar mixture over yams and bake in 350°F (175°C) oven (4-5 on the thermostat) for 45 minutes. Serves 6.

## BAKED BANANAS

12 small firm ripe bananas      6 tablespoons (3 oz./90 ml.)
melted butter.

Peel bananas. Arrange whole in baking dish. Pour melted butter over and bake 45 minutes in a 300°F (148°C) oven (2 on the thermostat). Serve as a vegetable.

NOTE: 4 ounces (125 ml.) rum and ½ cup (125 ml.) sugar can be added to this recipe. Serves 6.

## FRIED RIPE PLANTAINS

3 large ripe plantains      ½ cup (125 ml.) white sugar
Peanut oil      2 cups (500 ml.) hot water

When skin is black, plantains are ripe for frying. Peel off skin. Cut plantains in half, making three slices lengthwise in each, or slice in 1½-inch (4-cm.) rounds. In skillet with about ½ inch (1.5 cm.) hot oil, brown slices on both sides. Remove as they are browned, replacing with more plantains until all are cooked, using more oil if necessary. Put all browned slices back in skillet; sprinkle with sugar and pour in hot water. Cover closely, lower heat, and allow to cook 15 minutes or until water is absorbed. Serves 6.

# GREEN PLANTAIN CHIPS

3 large green plantains          Salt to taste
6 tablespoons (90 ml.) peanut oil


Peel skin from plantains. Slice rounds ½ inch (1.5 cm.) thick. In large skillet, in 3 tablespoons (45 ml.) hot oil, fry to light brown. Do not crowd. Remove from skillet and place on chopping board. With knife blade or mallet, flatten slices to half as thick. To skillet, add remaining oil and fry again to deep brown. Remove and drain on absorbent paper. Salt on both sides. Serve as vegetable or as hors d'oeuvre.

If desired, freeze flattened slices and fry the second time just before serving. Serves 6 as vegetable. Makes 40 slices for hors d'oeuvre.

# BROILED EGGPLANT

2 small firm eggplants          Salt and pepper
Olive oil (Melted butter or
  bacon drippings can also be
  used.)


Peel eggplants and slice rounds ½ inch (1.5 cm.) thick. Place slices in broiler pan. Sprinkle with salt and pepper and brush with oil. Broil 2½ inches (6.5 cm.) from heat for 5 minutes. Turn and broil on opposite side 5 more minutes. Serve at once. Serves 6.

## BLACK-EYED PEAS AND HAM HOCK

1 pound (450 g.) dried
  black-eyed peas
2 ham hocks
1 onion, chopped
6 cups (1.5 liters) water,
  approximately

Salt to taste
2 tablespoons (30 ml.) cooking
  oil or shortening
1 teaspoon (5 ml.) sage
6 drops Tabasco

Sort and wash peas. In soup kettle, put peas and ham hocks. Cover with water, and gently boil for 3 hours, adding water, if necessary. In skillet, sauté onions in oil or shortening and add to peas. Add seasoning and cook 15 minutes longer or until tender. Serves 6.

## STEWED OKRA, CORN, AND TOMATOES

1 pound (450 g.) fresh okra
4 ears fresh corn, or one 16-oz.
  (450-g.) can whole kernel corn
2 large tomatoes, or one 16-oz.
  (450-g.) can tomatoes
1 onion, minced
½ green pepper, chopped
1 teaspoon (5 ml.) salt

½ teaspoon (2.5 ml.) pepper
½ teaspoon (2.5 ml.) paprika
½ teaspoon (2.5 ml.) curry
  powder, optional
1 teaspoon (5 ml.) brown sugar
1 tablespoon (15 ml.) cooking oil
1 cup (250 ml.) water

Remove and discard stem ends from okra. Cut each pod into four slices. Cut kernels from ears of corn. Peel and slice tomatoes. In a heavy skillet, sauté onion in oil. Remove from skillet. Sauté okra until browned. Add tomatoes, onion, green pepper and all seasonings, and water. Bring to boil. Reduce heat and simmer 15 minutes. Add corn and simmer until tender. Serves 6.

# MIRLITONS STUFFED WITH HAM AND SHRIMP

6 medium mirlitons
½ pound (225 g.) raw shrimp,
  peeled, deveined, chopped
½ pound (225 g.) ground cooked
  ham
1 medium onion, coarsely
  chopped
1 large bunch green onions,
  chopped
4 parsley sprigs, chopped
3 celery tops and leaves,
  chopped

2 large garlic cloves, minced
½ teaspoon (2.5 ml.) salt
¼ teaspoon (1.25 ml.) thyme,
  ground
⅛ teaspoon (0.5 ml.) Cayenne
  pepper
½ cup (125 ml.) bacon drippings
1 cup (250 ml.) fresh white
  bread
1 egg, beaten

Drop mirlitons in boiling water to cover. Boil rapidly for about 40 minutes or until fork tender. Drain. Cool. Split in halves. Scoop out pulp, leaving shell intact, and invert shells on absorbent paper to drain. Discard seeds. Chop pulp. Sauté vegetables in bacon drippings until limp. Add ham and shrimp, stirring gently, and cook a few more minutes. Add reserved mirliton pulp, seasoning, and ¾ cup (175 ml.) bread crumbs. Mix well and cook a few more minutes. Remove from heat. Add egg. Cook 1 minute longer. Spoon mixture into mirliton shells. Sprinkle with leftover crumbs and dot with butter. Place shells in buttered dish. Cook in middle of 375°F (188°C) oven (4-5 on the thermostat) for about 20 to 30 minutes.

NOTE: The mirliton is a vegetable pear of the gourd family which is cultivated mainly in Louisiana, Latin America, and Algeria. Serves 6.

## CUSHAW

10 pounds (about 5 kg.) cushaw
2 cups (500 ml.) sugar
2 cups (500 ml.) water
2 oz. (56 g.) butter
1 teaspoon (5 ml.) ground ginger

½ teaspoon (2.5 ml.) ground cinnamon
½ teaspoon (2.5 ml.) ground cloves
Pinch salt

Cut cushaw into 4-inch (10-cm.) squares. Peel and seed. In covered saucepan, boil until fork tender. Drain if necessary. Add butter; mix to melt. Place in 2-inch (5-cm.) deep baking dish. Sprinkle with sugar and spices. Bake in 325°F (162°C) oven (3 on the thermostat) for 45 minutes.

NOTE: Serve hot as vegetable side dish. Especially good with pork and lamb. Will store very well in refrigerator for several weeks. Serves 6.

## SKILLET CABBAGE

4 cups (1 liter) shredded cabbage
1 green pepper, sliced julienne style
2 cups (500 ml.) diced celery

2 large onions, sliced
2 tomatoes, chopped
¼ cup (60 ml.) bacon drippings
2 teaspoons (10 ml.) sugar
Salt and pepper to taste

Combine ingredients in large skillet. Cover. Cook over medium heat 15 to 20 minutes, or until done to taste. Serves 6.

## BOILED BEETS AND GREENS

6 large or 12 medium beets      2 tablespoons (30 ml.) melted
butter

Cut stems at about 1 inch (2.5 cm.) from beets. Do not cut roots. Do not wash. Do not peel. Place beets in sauce pan and add just enough cold water to cover. Add:

1 teaspoon (5 ml.) salt      1 teaspoon (5 ml.) sugar

Cover and cook 25 to 50 minutes, according to size and freshness. When cooked, immediately drain. Peel with hands under running cold water. Cut roots. Add melted butter. Slice beets if large.

**GREENS**

Select greens. Wash well and drain. Put in saucepan with:

2 tablespoons (56 g.) butter      1 teaspoon (5 ml.) M.S.G.
1 teaspoon (5 ml.) salt      2 tablespoons water
1 teaspoon (5 ml.) sugar

Cook quickly for about 10 minutes. Fresh large beets can be prepared the same way and cooked in 300°F (148°C) oven (2 on the thermostat) for two hours. Serves 6.

## FRENCH FRIED BROCCOLI

2 pounds (1 kg.) fresh broccoli    2 tablespoons (30 ml.) water
3 cups (750 ml.) bread crumbs    Salt and pepper to taste
2 eggs, beaten    Cooking oil

Separate broccoli into pieces by slicing lengthwise. Do not remove stems. In large saucepan, place broccoli with enough salted water to cover, and slowly bring to boil. Boil rapidly for 5 minutes, and carefully remove from water, placing in colander. Refresh under cold water. Beat eggs and water together; add seasoning. Dip broccoli in egg mixture, then in bread crumbs until completely coated. In heavy skillet, place about 1 inch (2.5 cm.) cooking oil. Heat to 390°F (198°C). With slotted spoon, carefully lower broccoli into oil and fry until bread crumbs are golden. Remove and drain on absorbent paper. Serves 6.

## STUFFED CREOLE TOMATOES

6 creole tomatoes
3 tablespoons (43 g.) garlic
  butter

Bread crumbs
1½ teaspoons (7.5 ml.) sugar
Salt, pepper, parsley

Remove a ½-inch (1.5-cm.) slice from top of each tomato and chop. Scoop out most of pulp, and chop. Put a little salt, pepper, and sugar inside each tomato and turn upside down on absorbent paper to drain.

In small skillet, melt garlic butter. Add chopped slices of tomato and pulp. Cook quickly on high heat until most of juice has evaporated and chopped tomatoes are cooked. Add enough bread crumbs to form thick mixture. Add salt, pepper, sugar, and parsley. Mix, and stuff drained tomato shells. Dot with garlic butter and put in greased baking dish just large enough to hold tomatoes. Cook 10 minutes in 450°F (235°C) oven (6-7 on the thermostat). Put under broiler to brown. Serves 6.

## CHEESE GRITS CASSEROLE

1½ cups (375 ml.) hominy grits
  (Do not use quick cooking
  grits.)
6 cups (1.5 liters) boiling water
1½ teaspoon (7.5 ml.) salt
6 oz. (168 g.) sharp cheddar
  cheese, thinly sliced

¾ cup (175 ml.) milk
¾ cup (175 ml.) buttered bread
  crumbs
½ teaspoon (2.5 ml.) paprika
2 medium eggs, lightly beaten

In heavy saucepan, stir grits slowly into boiling salted water. Cook 5 minutes, stirring occasionally. Allow grits to cool. Mix well with beaten eggs. In greased 1½-quart (1.5-liter) baking dish, alternate layers of cooked grits and cheese. Pour milk over top. Sprinkle with bread crumbs and paprika. Bake in preheated slow oven (325°F/165°C) (3 on the thermostat) about 30 minutes. Serves 6.

# CORN PUDDING

17-oz. (463-g.) can creamed
corn, drained, liquid reserved
2 tablespoons (1 oz./28 g.) butter
2 tablespoons (30 ml.) flour
1 cup (250 ml.) evaporated milk
1 green pepper, finely chopped
1 pimento, chopped

1 tablespoon (15 ml.) sugar
2 eggs, separated
2 teaspoons (10 ml.) salt
4 tablespoons (60 ml.) melted
butter
Dash of black pepper

In a heavy skillet melt 2 tablespoons (28 g.) butter over medium heat. Remove from heat; add flour, blend, and cook a few minutes stirring constantly. Do not brown. Remove from heat and slowly add evaporated milk and reserved corn liquid. Return to heat; continue to cook, stirring until sauce is smooth and boiling. Add corn, green pepper, pimento, sugar, salt, and pepper. Stir until mixture returns to boil; reduce heat. Beat egg yolks well, add part to corn mixture, beat and reverse process. Cook, stirring until thickened. Remove from heat and cool. Beat egg whites with a pinch of salt until very stiff. Fold into corn mixture. Pour into an ungreased baking dish and drizzle melted butter on top. In a 325°F (160°C) oven (3 on the thermostat) bake for 10 minutes. Raise heat to 350°F (175°C) (4-5 on the thermostat) and bake 20 minutes more or until firm and top is lightly browned. Serves 6.

# Salads

## BOILED OKRA SALAD

1 pound (450 g.) whole fresh  
  medium-sized okra  
Lettuce

Olive oil and wine vinegar  
Salt and pepper to taste

In large saucepan, place okra in enough salted water to barely cover. Slowly bring okra to boil. Reduce heat and allow to simmer until tender but firm. Remove from heat and drain in colander. Refresh under cold water. Chill about 1 hour.

In salad bowl, make bed of lettuce. Put okra in center. Drizzle small amount of olive oil and vinegar. Toss okra lightly. Add salt and pepper. Toss again, making sure all is well coated. Serves 6.

## MUSHROOM SALAD

1½ pounds (650 g.) fresh white  
  mushroom caps  
2 hard-boiled eggs, chopped  
8 slices bacon, cooked and  
  crumbled

Plain croutons  
3 Boston lettuce leaves and  
  heart  
1 cup (250 ml.) vinaigrette

Wipe mushroom caps clean and slice thin. Divide lettuce leaves on plates. Shred lettuce hearts over leaves. Add mushrooms, eggs, bacon, and croutons. Pour vinaigrette of your choice over, or the following:

DRESSING  
2 egg yolks  
2 tablespoons (30 ml.)  
  mayonnaise  
2 tablespoons (30 ml.) lemon  
  juice

¼ cup (60 ml.) white wine  
  vinegar  
¾ cup (175 ml.) oil  
Salt and pepper

Mix egg yolks with mayonnaise. Slowly add lemon juice, vinegar, and seasonings. In a thin stream, stirring constantly, add the oil. Serves 6.

## WATERCRESS SALAD

2 bunches watercress
6 potatoes

3 hard-boiled eggs, chopped
Chopped parsley

Cut off and discard lower stems of watercress. Wash and shake dry. Boil potatoes until cooked but firm. Cool; peel and chop coarsely. Refrigerate, covered with absorbent paper until cold. Mix with watercress.

### VINAIGRETTE

½ teaspoon (2.5 ml.) salt
Large shake black pepper
2 tablespoons (30 ml.) seasoned vinegar or 1 tablespoon (15 ml.) seasoned vinegar and 1 tablespoon (15 ml.) lemon juice

4 to 6 tablespoons (60 to 90 ml.) olive oil
Dry mustard (optional)
Garlic (optional)
Chives (optional)

Mix salt, pepper, mustard or garlic if used, with vinegar or vinegar and lemon juice, until salt has dissolved. Slowly pour oil and beat briskly. Pour over potatoes and watercress. Mix well. Sprinkle with chopped eggs and parsley. Serve immediately. Serves 6.

## STRING BEAN SALAD

1½ pounds (650 g.) fresh string
  beans
1 gallon (4 liters) water with salt
  to taste

Sour cream salad dressing
Croutons

Rinse beans, remove strings and both ends, and snap in two. Place beans in colander. In large pot, boil water; submerge colander, and cook for 5 minutes. Remove, drain, and refresh under cold water. Refrigerate. Serve with sour cream dressing, and sprinkle croutons on top.

**DRESSING**
1 cup (250 ml.) sour cream
1 teaspoon (5 ml.) grated onion
1 teaspoon (5 ml.) celery seed
½ teaspoon (2.5 ml.) salt
½ teaspoon (2.5 ml.) sugar

¼ teaspoon (1.25 ml.) white
  pepper
1 teaspoon (5 ml.) vinegar or
  lemon juice

Beat sour cream until smooth. Add all other ingredients. Mix well. Serves 6.

## CUCUMBER SALAD (1)

3 small cucumbers
½ cup (125 ml.) heavy cream
5 green onions, chopped fine

Head of Boston lettuce
Salt and pepper

Peel and slice or dice cucumbers. Put in bowl with 2 teaspoons (10 ml.) salt. Mix and let stand at room temperature at least one hour. Drain and pat dry. Meanwhile, mix green onions, salt, pepper with cream. When ready to serve, shred lettuce, add cucumbers, and cream mixture. Mix well. This salad requires a good amount of pepper. Serves 6.

## CUCUMBER SALAD (2)

2 cucumbers
½ cup (125 ml.) lemon juice
1 cup (250 ml.) water
2 teaspoons (10 ml.) sugar

6 oz. (175 ml.) sour cream
Salt to taste
Lettuce

With table fork, score cucumbers skins deeply lengthwise several times. Slice very thin. In deep bowl, mix lemon juice, water, and sugar. Soak slices of cucumber in mixture. Refrigerate at least 12 hours. Drain and serve on lettuce leaf. Top with salted sour cream. Serves 6.

## JERUSALEM ARTICHOKE SALAD

1½ lbs. (650 g.) Jerusalem
    artichokes
Water
Salt
Chopped parsley

2 green onions, chopped fine
1 cup (250 ml.) mayonnaise or
    favorite salad dressing

Wash and peel Jerusalem artichokes. Cover with water. Add salt. Boil until tender. Drain and cool. Chop or slice thin. Add green onions. Mix. Add mayonnaise or salad dressing. Mix well. Sprinkle with parsley. Serves 6.

# Desserts

# BREAD PUDDING

8 slices stale bread in chunks
1 cup (250 ml.) light cream
1 cup (250 ml.) milk
1 cup (8 oz./225 g.) butter,
   softened

1 cup (250 ml.) sugar
2 teaspoons (10 ml.) rum
1 teaspoon (5 ml.) vanilla

Wet bread with cream and milk. Add sugar, rum, vanilla, and softened butter. Mix with rotary or electric beater until creamy. Pour into greased buttered pan. Bake in oven at 350°F (175°C) (4-5 on the thermostat) for 1 hour or until browned. Cool 5 minutes.

## TOPPING

3 egg whites
Pinch of salt

6 tablespoons (90 ml.) sugar

Beat egg whites and salt until stiff. Add sugar one tablespoon (15 ml.) at a time. Spread on cooled pudding. Put under broiler until golden brown.

## CUSTARD

1 cup (250 ml.) light cream
1 cup (250 ml.) milk
3 egg yolks
½ cup (125 ml.) sugar

3 tablespoons (45 ml.) whiskey,
   bourbon, or rye
1 teaspoon (5 ml.) vanilla

Bring milk and cream to boil. Beat egg yolks with sugar. Pour some hot milk in egg mixture; beat well and reverse procedure. Return to low heat and cook until slightly thickened and creamy. Add whiskey and vanilla and serve over pudding. Serves 6.

# RICE PUDDING

1 cup (250 ml.) rice
2 cups (500 ml.) light cream
2 cups (500 ml.) milk
1 cup (250 ml.) sugar
¼ teaspoon (1.25 ml.) salt

2 teaspoons (10 ml.) vanilla
5 egg yolks
1 cup (250 ml.) whipping cream

In top of double boiler, mix rice, light cream, milk, sugar, and salt. Cover and cook 1 to 1½ hours, stirring occasionally. Lightly mix egg yolks with vanilla, and slowly add to hot rice, stirring constantly. Cook a few minutes to thicken. Empty into bowl. Cover and refrigerate, stirring occasionally. Whip cream, and add to cold rice. May be served with strawberry or other fruit sauce, if desired. Serves 6.

# CHERRIES JUBILEE

Two 16-oz. (450-g.) cans pitted
  Bing cherries
2 tablespoons (30 ml.)
  cornstarch or arrowroot
  mixed with 2 tablespoons (30
  ml.) cold water

½ cup (125 ml.) Maraschino
  liqueur
6 large scoops vanilla ice cream
½ cup (125 ml.) Kirsch or
  brandy

Drain cherries and reserve liquid. In small saucepan, bring cherry liquid to simmer. Add cornstarch or arrowroot paste and cook, stirring, until sauce comes to boil and thickens. Cool to room temperature, then cover and set aside. When ready to serve, put ice cream in chilled individual dessert plates. In chafing dish, heat cherries, stirring constantly. Add Kirsch or brandy, Maraschino liqueur. Warm up a few minutes and flambé. Shake pan gently until flame dies. Stir in cherry sauce and heat thoroughly. Spoon cherries and sauce over ice cream. Serve immediately. Serves 6.

## BANANAS FOSTER

6 firm small ripe bananas,
  peeled and sliced in two
  lengthwise
6 large scoops vanilla ice cream
12 tablespoons (6 oz./168 g.)
  butter

¾ cup (175 ml.) brown sugar
Dash of cinnamon
¾ cup (175 ml.) banana liqueur
1 cup (250 ml.) rum

In chafing dish, flambé pan or large skillet, melt brown sugar and butter. Add bananas. Roll in syrup, sprinkle with cinnamon, and sauté until tender. Add banana liqueur and rum. Warm a few seconds and flambé. Baste bananas until flame dies. Serve two slices over ice cream and spoon sauce over. Serve immediately. Serves 6.

## BANANA MOUSSE

1 small package lemon-flavored
  gelatin
1 cup (250 ml.) boiling water

1 cup (250 ml.) whipping cream
2 ripe bananas, mashed

Dissolve gelatin in water. Cool until it starts to thicken. Whip cream very stiff. When gelatin is ready, add with bananas to cream. Whip until well blended. Refrigerate until set. Serve with the following custard.

### CUSTARD

½ cup (125 ml.) sugar
4 tablespoons (60 ml.) flour
¼ teaspoon (1.25 ml.) salt

1½ cups (375 ml.) milk
2 egg yolks
1 teaspoon (5 ml.) vanilla

In small saucepan, stir egg yolks with fork. Gradually add some milk. Add dry ingredients and mix well. Add rest of milk. Cook on top of stove on moderate heat until thick. Add vanilla. Cool. Spoon over mousse. Serves 6.

## AMBROSIA

6 large Louisiana navel oranges
1 cup (250 ml.) freshly grated
  coconut
Powdered sugar

½ cup (125 ml.) candied
  cherries, sliced, or
  Maraschino cherries
2 oz. (60 ml.) Kirsch or
  Cointreau

Peel oranges and discard membrane covering orange sections. Place sections in bowl. Add coconut, cherries, Kirsch or Cointreau, and mix. Sprinkle with small amount powdered sugar. Chill for 2 hours. Serves 6.

## FRESH PINEAPPLE WITH CREAM CHEESE AND PECANS

1 large fresh pineapple
8-oz. (226-g.) package
  Philadelphia cream cheese
½ cup (125 ml.) chopped pecans
1 cup (250 ml.) mayonnaise

½ cup (125 ml.) pineapple juice
½ teaspoon (2.5 ml.) cinnamon
1 teaspoon (5 ml.) powdered
  sugar

Peel, core, and cube large fresh pineapple, and place in large bowl. Sprinkle with enough powdered sugar to coat and sweeten. Chill about 4 hours.

Soften cream cheese and make balls about 1 inch (2.5 cm.) in diameter. Roll in chopped pecans and chill about 30 minutes or until cold and firm.

**SAUCE**

Drain pineapple and reserve ½ cup (125 ml.) juice. Mix in mayonnaise, adding sugar and cinnamon. Blend well. Into 6 dessert bowls, divide pineapple and cheese balls. Serve with mayonnaise sauce. Serves 6.

## WATERMELON AND CHAMPAGNE

1 large watermelon        1 bottle (1 liter) dry champagne

Plug large ripe cold watermelon. Pour bottle of champagne in opening. Replace plug. Refrigerate overnight. Slice watermelon crosswise and serve. Serves 8 to 10.

## PRALINES

2 cups (500 ml.) dark brown
  sugar
1 cup (250 ml.) white sugar
1 cup (250 ml.) water
1 cup (250 ml.) whipping
  cream

3 cups (750 ml.) pecan halves
1 tablespoon (15 ml.) vanilla
½ teaspoon (2.5 ml.) salt

In heavy skillet over medium heat, combine both sugars, water, and salt. Dissolve sugar well. Add cream. Continue to cook at slight boil, stirring constantly, until soft ball appears, or 240°F (115°C) on candy thermometer. Remove from heat and beat in vanilla and pecans. Drop by tablespoons on greased marble slab or waxed paper to harden. Yield: 1 doz. large pralines.

## PECAN PIE

1 cup (250 ml.) brown sugar
2 tablespoons (30 ml.) flour
1 tablespoon (14 g.) butter
1 cup (250 ml.) light corn syrup
3 eggs, beaten

¼ teaspoon (1.25 ml.) salt
1 teaspoon (5 ml.) vanilla
1 cup (250 ml.) pecan halves
9-inch (23-cm.) unbaked pie
  shell

Cream butter with mixed sugar and flour; add syrup and eggs. Beat mixture until frothy. Add salt, vanilla, and pecan halves. Pour into unbaked pie shell. Bake 40 minutes at 325°F (165°C) (3 on the thermostat). Yield: One 9-inch (23-cm.) pie.

## MOLASSES PIE

3 eggs
2 tablespoons (30 ml.)
  all-purpose flour
¼ cup (2 oz./56 g.) soft butter
½ cup (125 ml.) sugar
½ teaspoon (2.5 ml.) allspice
⅛ teaspoon (0.5 ml.) nutmeg

1 teaspoon (5 ml.) baking soda
  soda
¼ teaspoon (1.25 ml.) salt
¾ cup (175 ml.) dark molasses
9-inch (23-cm.) unbaked
  piecrust
Whipped cream

Beat eggs slightly. Add flour, softened but not melted butter, sugar, allspice, nutmeg, and salt. Beat until well blended. In saucepan over medium heat, bring molasses to boil. Add soda. Cook, stirring constantly, until foam dies down. Cool, and add to egg mixture, mixing well. Pour into piecrust and bake at 300°F (148°C) (2 on the thermostat) about 30 minutes. Top with whipped cream. Yield: One 9-inch (23-cm.) pie.

## CALAS

1 cup (250 ml.) cooked rice
2 cups (500 ml.) sifted flour
1½ cups (375 ml.) water
2 teaspoons (10 ml.) baking
  powder
2 tablespoons (30 ml.) sugar
½ teaspoon (2.5 ml.) salt

1 teaspoon (5 ml.) vanilla
  extract
2 eggs
Cooking oil
Powdered sugar or Louisiana
  cane syrup

Beat eggs and sugar together with vanilla until bright yellow and foamy. Add water and beat well. In mixing bowl, add baking powder and salt to sifted flour. Add to egg mixture, blending well with wire whisk. Add rice, making sure all kernels are well coated. Divide dough into six portions. Moisten hands with a little cooking oil. Gently form six firm balls. Set aside on waxed paper.

In heavy skillet, heat about 1 inch (2.5 cm.) oil to 390°F (198°C). With slotted spoon, slowly lower rice balls into oil and fry until a rich golden crust appears, turning to keep from burning. Serve at once with powdered sugar or Louisiana cane syrup. Serves 6.

## BEIGNETS

3 cups (750 ml.) plain flour  
2 tablespoons (30 ml.) cooking oil  
2 tablespoons (30 ml.) sugar  
1 cup (250 ml.) scalded milk  
1 teaspoon (5 ml.) salt  

½ teaspoon (2.5 ml.) each nutmeg and cinnamon  
1 envelope dry yeast (¼ oz./9 g.)  
1 egg, beaten  
Oil for deep frying  
Powdered sugar  

Pour milk in large bowl with cooking oil and sugar. Blend well and cool to 105-110°F (40-41°C). Add dry yeast; stir to dissolve. Sift flour, salt, and spices together and add half to yeast mixture. Beat in egg and add remaining flour mixture. Form large ball. Cover and allow to rise to double. Punch down and knead gently until elastic. On floured board, roll out dough to ¼-inch (6-mm.) thickness. Cut into 2-inch (5-cm.) squares. Cover and allow to rise again for 45 minutes. Fill deep fryer with 3 inches (8 cm.) oil. Heat to 375°F (190°C). Drop in squares, cooking until light golden, and turn. Remove with slotted spoon to absorbent paper to drain. Dust with good quantity powdered sugar. Serve hot. Yield: 24 doughnuts.

## PRINCESS CUP

2 cups (500 ml.) fresh fruit in season  
1 quart (1 liter) vanilla ice cream  

2 tablespoons (30 ml.) Cointreau  
6 old-fashioned glasses (12 oz./375 ml.)  

Prepare fruit in usual manner. Fill glasses ⅓ full with fruit. Put large scoop of ice cream in each glass. Top with liqueur. Serves 6.

# FIG ICE CREAM

4 cups (1 liter) fresh whole
  peeled figs
1 cup (250 ml.) superfine sugar
⅛ teaspoon (0.5 ml.) salt
6 large egg yolks

2 cups (500 ml.) milk, scalded
2 cups (500 ml.) whipping cream
2 teaspoons (10 ml.) vanilla

Beat sugar, salt, and egg yolks until light yellow. In double boiler, place egg mixture and slowly add milk, beating with wire whisk until mixture thickens and coats wires. Remove from water and cool 10 minutes. Strain. Add heavy cream and vanilla. Carefully fold in figs, keeping them as whole as possible. Freeze in 2-quart (2-liter) hand-turned or electric ice cream freezer. Yield: 2 quarts (2 liters).

# FROZEN CREOLE CREAM CHEESE ICE CREAM

3 cups (750 ml.) Creole cream
  cheese*
2 cups (500 ml.) whipping cream
14-oz. (420-ml.) can condensed
  milk

1 teaspoon (5 ml.) vanilla
3 egg whites, beaten stiff
⅛ teaspoon (0.5 ml.) baking
  soda

Blend Creole cream cheese, and cream with wire whisk until creamy. Force mixture through colander until smooth. Add condensed milk and beat thoroughly. If mixture is too sour, add small amount of sugar. Add vanilla and fold in egg whites. Pour into 2-quart (2-liter) hand-turned or electric ice cream freezer. Turn until frozen. Yield: About 1¾ quarts (1.75 liters).

  *See #114.

## JELLY ROLL

3 eggs, beaten
1 cup (250 ml.) sugar
5 tablespoons (75 ml.) water
1 teaspoon (5 ml.) vanilla
1 cup (250 ml.) flour

1 teaspoon (5 ml.) baking
  powder
¼ teaspoon (1.25 ml.) salt
16 oz. (450 g.) strawberry jelly
Powdered sugar

To beaten eggs, gradually add sugar, water, and vanilla. Sift together flour, baking powder, and salt, and add to egg mixture. Beat until smooth. Grease and flour a 15½ x 10½-inch (39 x 26 cm.) jelly roll pan. Pour in mixture. Bake in 375°F (190°C) oven (5 on the thermostat) just until cake tests done—12 to 15 minutes. Loosen edges and immediately turn upside down on cloth towel sprinkled with powdered sugar. Spread cake at once with jelly and roll up, beginning at short end. Wrap in towel until cool. Unwrap and slice roll. Serves 10.

## PANCAKE LAYERED CAKE

2 cups (500 ml.) sifted flour
2 large eggs
1½ cups (375 ml.) milk
4 teaspoons (20 ml.) baking
  powder
1 teaspoon (5 ml.) sugar
3 tablespoons (45 ml.) melted
  butter

¼ teaspoon (1.25 ml.) salt
4 to 5 different leftover
  preserves, jellies, or
  conserves
Powdered sugar or cane syrup

In bowl, sift flour, sugar, baking powder, and salt. Beat eggs and milk together and blend into flour mixture until smooth. Add melted butter and blend well. On large hot griddle with enough butter to coat, pour enough batter to make 8-inch (20-cm.) pancake. Bake until golden and turn. Remove pancake to serving platter. Coat with first kind of jelly, preserve, or conserve. Make another 8-inch (20-cm.) pancake, and when cooked, place on top of first, using another kind of jelly, conserve, or preserve to coat. Continue in this fashion until all batter has been baked and layers are as high as you desire. Either dust with powdered sugar or pour cane syrup over layers. Slice as you would cake. Serve hot. Serves 6.

## WHITE FRUIT CAKE

1 pound (450 g.) crystallized
citron, cut fine
2 pounds (900 g.) golden raisins
1 pound (450 g.) whole pecans
1 pound (450 g.) crystallized
whole cherries
1 pound (450 g.) crystallized
pineapple, cut in chunks
1 pound (450 g.) butter
4 cups (1 liter) sifted flour,
divided in half
2 cups (500 ml.) white sugar
2 teaspoons (10 ml.) baking
powder

½ teaspoon (2.5 ml.) baking
soda
6 large eggs
2 tablespoons (30 ml.) fresh
grated nutmeg
Mix together:
1 teaspoon (5 ml.) almond
extract
2 tablespoons (30 ml.) vanilla
extract
1 cup (250 ml.) brandy or white
rum

In a bowl, mix half the sifted flour with fruit and pecans until they are well coated, and set aside. In mixing bowl, cream butter and sugar until golden and fluffy. Add eggs one at a time until well beaten. Combine other half of flour with baking powder, soda, and nutmeg. Blend into creamed butter, alternating with brandy or rum mixture. When batter is well mixed, add coated fruit and pecans.

In 9-inch (23-cm.) tube pan, make brown paper liner to fit. Grease all metal sides generously with solid shortening. Grease both sides of paper liner and press liner firmly to pan. Next, make waxed paper liner to cover brown liner and press firmly in place. Pour in batter. Place tube pan in another pan, and fill that pan with enough water to come half way up sides of tube pan. Cover batter pan with sheet of aluminum foil and seal securely. Place both pans in 275°F (132°C) oven (1 on the thermostat) and bake for 3½ hours. Remove from oven, and remove batter pan from water pan. Uncover. Reset oven for 325°F (160°C) (2 on the thermostat). Replace batter pan in oven. Bake for 30 to 40 minutes until brown on top. Remove from oven. Cool. Unmold carefully. Allow to cool thoroughly before storing. A week or so of aging improves cake. A small amount of whiskey or brandy can be poured on top to moisten and improve flavor. Yield: 5-pound (2.25-kg.) fruit cake.

## MOLASSES PECAN COOKIES

½ cup (4 oz./113 g.) butter
½ cup (125 ml.) brown sugar
2 eggs
½ cup (125 ml.) New Orleans
   dark molasses
1½ cups (375 ml.) sifted plain
   flour

¼ teaspoon (1.25 ml.) cinnamon
½ teaspoon (2.5 ml.) salt
½ teaspoon (2.5 ml.) baking
   soda
1½ cups (375 ml.) pecans,
   chopped fine

Cream butter and sugar; add eggs, one at a time, beating well. Add molasses. Blend well. Add flour, cinnamon, salt, and baking soda. Mix well. Add 1 cup (250 ml.) pecans. Mix well again. Drop by teaspoons on greased cookie sheet about 1½ inches (4 cm.) apart. Sprinkle tops with remaining ½ cup (125 ml.) pecans. Bake in 350°F (165°C) oven (3 on the thermostat) about 10 to 12 minutes. Remove at once. Cool. Yield: 50 cookies.

## DATE SQUARES

1 cup (250 ml.) light brown
   sugar
¾ cup (6 oz./168 g.) butter

1¾ cups (425 ml.) oatmeal
1¾ cups (425 ml.) flour
1 teaspoon (5 ml.) baking soda

Crumble all ingredients with hands or pastry blender until all are blended. Set aside.

**FILLING**

1 lb. (450 g.) pitted dates
1 cup (250 ml.) light brown
   sugar

1 tablespoon (14 g.) butter
1½ cups (375 ml.) hot water

In a saucepan mix all ingredients; over medium heat boil until thick, stirring occasionally. In an 8x8-inch (22x22-cm.) square pan spread half the oatmeal mixture, pressing firmly with hands. Cover with date mixture and other half of the oatmeal mixture. Bake in a preheated 375°F (190°C) oven (5 on the thermostat) for 45 minutes or until top is golden. Yield: 24 squares.

## GINGER SNAPS

3½ cups (875 ml.) flour
2 teaspoons (10 ml.) baking
  powder
¾ teaspoon (3.75 ml.) baking
  soda
1 teaspoon (5 ml.) salt

3 teaspoons (15 ml.) ginger
Few grains Cayenne
¾ cup (6 oz./168 g.) butter
¾ cup (175 ml.) sugar
¾ cup (175 ml.) molasses
2 tablespoons (30 ml.) water

Cream butter and sugar. Add molasses, water, and all the dry ingredients. Mix well. On a piece of waxed paper make small rolls with the mixture. Refrigerate 24 hours. Thinly slice and bake on a buttered cookie sheet 10 to 12 minutes in a 375°F (190°C) oven (5 on the thermostat). Yield: 5 dozen.

## LACE COOKIES

½ cup (4 oz./113 g.) butter
½ cup (125 ml.) molasses
¾ cup (175 ml.) powdered sugar

1 cup (250 ml.) flour
1 tablespoon (15 ml.) rum

Heat butter and sugar until well melted. Add molasses; mix well and let cool. Add flour and mix again. Drop on an ungreased cookie sheet by ¼ teaspoons (1.25 ml.) 3 to 4 inches (8 to 10 cm.) apart. Bake in an oven 375°F (190°C) (5 on the thermostat) about 8 minutes or until edges are golden. Cool a few seconds. Remove with a spatula and cool on a wire rack. Yield: 5 dozen.

# Miscellaneous

## PO-BOYS

1 large loaf New Orleans
  French bread (approx. 36
  inches or about 1 meter)
36 large oysters

Cooking oil
Corn meal
Salt and pepper
Sliced lettuce and tomatoes

At least ½ hour before using, drain oysters. Flour with corn meal, salt, and pepper. In large kettle, pour 3 inches (7.5 cm.) oil. Heat to 390°F (198°C). Gently lower oysters and deep fry until golden. Drain on absorbent paper and keep warm. Slice bread lengthwise. Arrange lettuce and tomatoes on bottom slice. Add oysters and cover with top slice. Slice loaf into six equal parts. Serve with mayonnaise or tomato ketchup.

NOTE: If Shrimp Po-Boy is served, use:

36 fresh, peeled, deveined,
  medium shrimp
1 egg beaten with salt and

pepper and 1 tablespoon (15
  ml.) water

Dip shrimp in egg mixture. Dredge in bread crumbs. Deep fry in same manner as oysters. Assemble Po-Boy as above. Leftover cold roast beef can be used in same manner. Serves 6.

## PAIN PERDU

2 eggs, well beaten
1 cup (250 ml.) milk
1 tablespoon (15 ml.) sugar
Pinch of salt
¼ teaspoon (1.25 ml.) vanilla
½ teaspoon (2.5 ml.) cinnamon
with 2 teaspoons (10 ml.)
sugar (optional)

2 tablespoons (1 oz./28 g.) butter
2 tablespoons (30 ml.) oil
6 slices white bread or 6 slices
stale French bread

In bowl, combine milk, beaten eggs, sugar, and vanilla. Mix thoroughly. If using stale French bread, soak a few minutes. If using sliced bread, slightly toast and soak just before frying. Melt butter in heavy skillet, add oil, and fry bread, one or two slices at a time, on each side until golden brown. If used, sprinkle with cinnamon and sugar mixture and serve with cane syrup. Serves 6.

## LOUISIANA PECAN WAFFLES

2 cups (500 ml.) sifted flour
4 teaspoons (20 ml.) baking
powder
½ teaspoon (2.5 ml.) salt
1 tablespoon (15 ml.) sugar

1½ cups (375 ml.) milk
3 large eggs, separated
4 tablespoons (60 ml.) melted
butter
1 cup (250 ml.) chopped pecans

Beat egg yolks into milk. Sift together flour, baking powder, sugar, and salt; add dry ingredients to milk and eggs, mixing thoroughly to remove lumps. Add melted butter and blend well again. Beat egg whites until stiff. Fold in pecans and add egg whites to batter. Heat waffle iron. Pour enough batter to bake proper-sized waffle. Bake until iron stops steaming and waffle is golden brown. Yield: 12 small or 6 large waffles.

## BANANA FRITTERS

2 large very ripe bananas,
mashed
1 cup (250 ml.) sifted flour
2 teaspoons (10 ml.) baking
powder
1 large egg

¼ cup (60 ml.) milk
1 teaspoon (5 ml.) sugar
1 teaspoon (5 ml.) vanilla
extract
Pinch of salt
Cooking oil

In mixing bowl, place flour, sugar, baking powder, and salt. Beat egg, milk, and vanilla until well blended. Add egg mixture to flour mixture and blend well. Add mashed bananas and blend.

In heavy skillet, place about 1 inch (2.5 cm.) oil and bring to 375°F (190°C). Drop spoonfuls of mixture in hot oil and fry until golden brown, turning to get even color. Remove from oil and drain on absorbent paper. Sprinkle fritters with powdered sugar. Serves 6.

## BASIC BROWN ROUX

The trick in making a good brown roux is as follows:

Put equal parts of plain white flour and cooking oil or solid shortening in a cold cast-iron skillet. Blend together the two ingredients with a wooden spoon. Turn heat to the very lowest possible setting. These first two steps are important and must be followed to produce the best results. Stir until mixture begins to bubble, about 5 minutes. Continue to stir; do not stop. In about 30 minutes a good brown color will begin to appear. If it is coming up too fast, remove the skillet from the heat and allow to cool slightly, stirring constantly. This will slow down the browning process. When a rich brown color appears, remove from heat; cool a few seconds; then slowly pour into the skillet the desired liquid.

## CREOLE CREAM CHEESE
## MASTER RECIPE

3 half-gallons (5.6 liters)        1 quart (1 liter) buttermilk
pasteurized whole milk


Place whole milk and buttermilk in large bowl and cover with cloth. In about 24 hours, milk mixture will separate from whey, leaving curds. Line colander with 6 thicknesses cheesecloth. Place in bowl and pour curds in, allowing whey to drain into bowl. When thick cheese occurs, pour into container and refrigerate. Yield: About 1 quart (1 liter).

NOTE: Do not use homogenized milk

## CANDIED GRAPEFRUIT, LEMON, OR ORANGE PEEL

Grapefruit, orange, or lemon        Sugar and honey
   peels                            Water


Remove all membranes so that only peeling remains. Cut into julienne strip. Put in saucepan with enough water to cover. Boil 5 minutes. Drain and repeat process twice, each time using fresh water. Cool. Weigh peels and weigh equal amount of sugar and honey, using half of each. Put in saucepan. Add ⅓ cup (80 ml.) water for every cup (250 ml.) honey-sugar mixture. Simmer 20 minutes or until peels are glazed. Drain 24 hours. On plate or piece of waxed paper, spread ½ cup (125 ml.) sugar and roll each strip in it. Place on cookie sheet to dry.

## LOUISIANA FIG CHUTNEY

4 cups (1 liter) whole fresh figs,
   washed
⅓ cup (80 ml.) sugar
⅓ cup (80 ml.) water

¼ teaspoon (1.25 ml.) each:
   ground ginger, allspice,
   cinnamon, and cloves
1 lemon, cut in small pieces

In saucepan, place all ingredients and figs. Over medium heat, bring to boil, stirring frequently. Lower heat and allow to cook for 5 minutes or until thick brown syrup appears. Cool. Store in containers in refrigerator or freeze for future use. Yield: 1-pint (500-ml.) jar.

NOTE: Day old figs that have become overripe may be used up in chutney.

## HOT PEPPER JELLY

¼ cup (60 ml.) seeded and
   minced red hot peppers
¾ cup (175 ml.) seeded and
   minced bell peppers
1½ cups (375 ml.) cider vinegar
6½ cups (1 liter plus 625 ml.)
   sugar

6-oz. (175-ml.) bottle fruit pectin
Green food coloring
5 Mason jars, sterilized
   (8-oz./250-ml.)

Place minced peppers in large saucepan. Add sugar and vinegar. Mix well. Bring to boil and cook 10 minutes. Add pectin and bring to rolling boil for 1 minute. Add food coloring. Cool slightly and put in glass jars. Yield: About five 8-oz. (250-ml.) jars.

# BANANA JELLY

6 ripe bananas (large)          Lemon juice
Water

Peel and cut bananas in chunks. Place in saucepan; add water and lemon juice to level of fruit. Cook uncovered over low heat until moisture is drawn from fruit, then increase heat to moderate. Cook 20 minutes. Remove from heat and transfer to jelly bag. A jelly bag is made from a piece of flannel or several thicknesses of cheesecloth. Wet bag, wring it, and place it over colander or hang it on peg. Do not press bag. When all banana juice has been extracted, you are ready to make jelly. Reserve juice.

## JELLY

1 cup (250 ml.) reserved banana          ¾ cup (175 ml.) sugar
  juice

Place banana juice in large enamel or stainless steel pan. Simmer 5 minutes. Skim off any froth that forms. Add sugar. Stir until sugar is dissolved. Keep simmering, but stop stirring. Cook just to point of jellying, about 10 minutes after sugar is added. To test for jellying, place small amount of jelly in spoon, cool slightly, and let drop back into pan from side of spoon. Two large drops will form along edge of spoon, one on either side. When these two drops come together and sheet off (216-220°F/100°C), the jelly point has been reached. Remove from heat and allow to cool. Yield: 1 pint jar (500 ml.).

## PICKLED SWEET AND SOUR MIRLITON RELISH

18 or 20 mirlitons
6 large onions, sliced thin
2 carrots, sliced thin
1 cup (250 ml.) salt
6 cups (1.5 liters) vinegar
6 cups (1.5 liters) white sugar
⅓ cup (80 ml.) mustard seed

1½ tablespoons (22.5 ml.) celery
  seeds
¼ teaspoon (1.25 ml.) Cayenne
  pepper
8 to 10 one-quart (1 liter) Mason
  jars, sterilized

Cut mirlitons in half. Remove seeds. Peel and slice very thin. Soak with onions and carrots in stone or enamel container with salt and water to cover for 3 to 5 hours. Drain, and discard water. In saucepan, combine vinegar, sugar, and spices. Simmer for 5 minutes. Add mirliton mixture. Bring just to simmer and hold for 5 to 10 minutes. Jar and seal at once. Yield: 8 to 10 one-quart (1-liter) jars

NOTE: Freezes well.

### FAVORITE NEW ORLEANS RECIPES

_____ English edition @ $4.95
_____ French edition @ $6.95
_____ Spanish edition @ $6.95
_____ Trilingual edition @ $12.95

Please send me the edition(s) checked. Enclosed is _____ including $1.50 each for postage and handling. Louisiana residents please add applicable sales tax.

Name_____

Street_____

City_____State_____Zip_____

Pelican Publishing Co.   P.O. Box 189   Gretna, LA 70054

---

### FAVORITE NEW ORLEANS RECIPES

_____ English edition @ $4.95
_____ French edition @ $6.95
_____ Spanish edition @ $6.95
_____ Trilingual edition @ $12.95

Please send me the edition(s) checked. Enclosed is _____ including $1.50 each for postage and handling. Louisiana residents please add applicable sales tax.

Name_____

Street_____

City_____State_____Zip_____

Pelican Publishing Co.   P.O. Box 189   Gretna, LA 70054

---

### FAVORITE NEW ORLEANS RECIPES

_____ English edition @ $4.95
_____ French edition @ $6.95
_____ Spanish edition @ $6.95
_____ Trilingual edition @ $12.95

Please send me the edition(s) checked. Enclosed is _____ including $1.50 each for postage and handling. Louisiana residents please add applicable sales tax.

Name_____

Street_____

City_____State_____Zip_____

Pelican Publishing Co.   P.O. Box 189   Gretna, LA 70054

## FAVORITE NEW ORLEANS RECIPES

_____ English edition @ $4.95
_____ French edition @ $6.95
_____ Spanish edition @ $6.95
_____ Trilingual edition @ $12.95

Please send me the edition(s) checked. Enclosed is _____ including $1.50 each for postage and handling. Louisiana residents please add applicable sales tax.

Name_____

Street_____

City_____State_____Zip_____

Pelican Publishing Co.   P.O. Box 189   Gretna, LA 70054

---

## FAVORITE NEW ORLEANS RECIPES

_____ English edition @ $4.95
_____ French edition @ $6.95
_____ Spanish edition @ $6.95
_____ Trilingual edition @ $12.95

Please send me the edition(s) checked. Enclosed is _____ including $1.50 each for postage and handling. Louisiana residents please add applicable sales tax.

Name_____

Street_____

City_____State_____Zip_____

Pelican Publishing Co.   P.O. Box 189   Gretna, LA 70054

---

## FAVORITE NEW ORLEANS RECIPES

_____ English edition @ $4.95
_____ French edition @ $6.95
_____ Spanish edition @ $6.95
_____ Trilingual edition @ $12.95

Please send me the edition(s) checked. Enclosed is _____ including $1.50 each for postage and handling. Louisiana residents please add applicable sales tax.

Name_____

Street_____

City_____State_____Zip_____

Pelican Publishing Co.   P.O. Box 189   Gretna, LA 70054